'George Herbert! What poet is w[...]
Richard Harries! Who else today[...]
This profound little gem will dr[...]
poetry and life.'
**David F. Ford OBE**, Regius Professor of Divinity Emeritus, University of Cambridge, England

'If you are a person who struggles to access or articulate the deep emotions of faith, then this book will be of interest. With insight and sensitivity, Harries explores the way in which Herbert's poetry mirrors the ups and downs of our own faith journeys, and helps the modern mind to connect with themes, such as sin, judgement and woundedness, that may seem outdated. *Wounded I Sing* is an Advent song for the soul which, with all the intensity of the minor key, plumbs the depths of sorrow but emerges rejoicing.'
**Guli Francis-Dehqani**, Bishop of Chelmsford, England

'This is a book of extraordinary beauty – compelling, elegant, profound, spiritual and moving. For those who find poetry difficult, this is an excellent way in; for those who know their George Herbert well, there is much that they can learn. Richard Harries has written a book that uses poetry as a vehicle for preparation (whether for Advent or for any other season). It will become a spiritual classic of our time.'
**Ian S. Markham**, President of Virginia Theological Seminary and of General Theological Seminary, USA

'Like the season of Advent, Herbert's poems are often in the vocative. They shout out to God for some repair, forgiveness or answer. To bring them together is very helpful and, placed together with the creative curation and spiritual intelligence of Richard Harries, we are given a valuable companion. In the world, Advent is at risk. This book ensures that people of faith will know it and draw from it, as the poetic well of wisdom and hope it is for the human spirit.'

**Mark Oakley**, Dean of Southwark Cathedral, England, and author of *My Sour-Sweet Days*

**Richard Harries** is a Fellow of the Royal Society of Literature and the author of more than thirty books, most recently *The Beauty and the Horror: Searching for God in a suffering world* (2016), *Haunted by Christ: Modern writers and the struggle for faith* (2018), *Seeing God in Art: The Christian faith in 30 images* (2020), *Hearing God in Poetry: Fifty poems for Lent and Easter* (2021), and *Majesty: Reflections on the life of Christ with Queen Elizabeth II*, all published by SPCK. His autobiography, *The Shaping of a Soul: A life taken by surprise*, is published by John Hunt. He was Bishop of Oxford from 1987 to 2006 and is a member of the House of Lords (Lord Harries of Pentregarth).

# WOUNDED I SING

From Advent to Christmas
with George Herbert

Richard Harries

First published in Great Britain in 2024

SPCK
SPCK Group
Studio 101
The Record Hall
16–16A Baldwin's Gardens
London EC1N 7RJ
www.spckpublishing.co.uk

*British Library Cataloguing-in-Publication Data*
A catalogue record for this book is available from the British Library

ISBN 978–0–281–08942–0
eBook ISBN 978–0–281–08949–9

1 3 5 7 9 10 8 6 4 2

Typeset by Manila Typesetting Company
First printed in Great Britain by Clays Ltd

eBook by Manila Typesetting Company

Produced on paper from sustainable sources

For Christine and Bill Risbero

# Contents

## Week 1
### WINNING THE HEART

## Week 2
### WELCOME

# Acknowledgements

I would particularly like to thank John Drury for his wonderful book
*Music at Midnight: The life and poetry of George Herbert* and Ann
Pasternak Slater who nearly thirty years ago kindly gave me a copy
of her edition of *The Complete English Works of George Herbert* in
the Everyman's Library series. I have followed her edition for layout
and spelling of the poems. Anyone who wishes to study Herbert further cannot do better than delve into these two books. I would also
like to thank Christabel Gairdner, whose eagle eyes helped iron out
infelicities.

# Author's note

The conventional picture of George Herbert is of a saintly priest quietly going about his duties in a country parish. But Herbert was a passionate man, full of ambition, who experienced fierce inner conflict. It was out of this struggle to bring his life under God that his poetry came. So, as he wrote, 'Wounded I sing.'

# INTRODUCTION

# George Herbert in his time

## England in the early seventeenth century

The early seventeenth century, in which George Herbert lived most of his life, was a good time to be alive. There was a sense of excitement as new lands were explored to the East and West, comparable to the way many people felt fifty years ago about the first landings on the moon. In 1595 Sir Walter Raleigh had voyaged west to Guiana and Trinidad and written a book about it. In 1620 the first colonies were set up in New England. In his long, early poem The Church Militant, Herbert rejoiced that the Christian faith was following the sun westwards. It was a confident vision. The world was expanding, the faith was growing.

Although The Royal Society was not founded until 1660, science was already developing, notably in William Harvey's work on the circulation of the blood and in the work of Francis Bacon who set out the basic principles of scientific method. It was not just the world that was expanding; so was knowledge. There was a sense of intellectual as well as physical exploration and excitement.

Above all, England was *relatively* peaceful. The tumults of the Reformation period, with successive Protestant and Catholic monarchs and ensuing martyrdoms on both sides, had settled down into the reigns of Elizabeth I and James I. The Church of England had steadied itself as a *via media* between the two extremes as a Church of the Reformation that drew on its Catholic heritage. At the same time, the Civil War which broke out in 1642 still lay ahead, after Herbert's death.

It was therefore a time that allowed for balance, rationality and elegance. This was reflected in the classical proportions of its Palladian architecture, as in the design of the Queen's House at Greenwich by Inigo Jones, which was begun in 1616 and the Banqueting Hall in Whitehall, begun in 1619, also by Jones.

At the same time, the English language had never been richer, as evidenced in both Shakespeare, who died in 1616, and the King James Version of the Bible, which was published in 1611. On the continent it was the time of Pascal, Montaigne and Racine.

George Herbert was born in 1593 and died at the age of thirty-nine in 1633. This short period encompassed the reigns of three monarchs, for Queen Elizabeth I died in 1603 and James in 1625, when he was succeeded by Charles I. In the spring of 1603, when Herbert was about ten, Queen Elizabeth lay dying. As has been written, 'Few moments in English history have been more hungry for the future, its mercurial possibilities and its hope of richness.'[1] The country had become tired and fed up in the last years of the Queen's reign. It was ready for something different, something new.

King James VI of Scotland, who ruled as James I of England from 1603 to 1625, had had a terrible childhood in Scotland without his mother, Mary Queen of Scots, from whom he had been separated, and at the mercy of the warring Scottish magnates. But he was a peacemaker who kept Britain out of the Thirty Years' War that devastated so much of Europe and did his best to avoid a war with Spain. Above all, he wanted to unite the British people in their religion. To this end he summoned a great conference at Hampton Court in 1604. What came out of this was the decision to produce a new authorised version of the Bible. More widely, although James would have nothing to do with dissenters who wanted to set up their own congregations, nor with Catholic revolutionaries, outside these extremes he wanted to include the broad range of Protestant opinion and be less repressive towards loyal Catholics. He kept the Church of England a broad Church. The Gunpowder Plot occurred in 1605, the third attempt on the life of James but, given the nature of the times, James's genuine desire to unite his people was relatively successful.

So in some respects it was a good time to live, though of course there were no anaesthetics and child mortality was high. A quarter of all children died before the age of ten. In the slums it could be three times that number. Life expectancy was thirty-five years. London, by which is meant mainly the City of London, was crowded, dirty and unhealthy. Houses were close to one another, the streets for the most part unpaved and oozing with mud and filth. One house, a former palace, was subdivided into eight thousand dwellings. Fewer than half the houses had their own kitchen and almost none their own oven. It was into this rank, unhealthy mass that plague struck in 1603, the year of James's coronation. The normal population of London, 140,000, was swelled by 100,000 visitors.

The seventeenth century is well known for the Great Plague of 1665–66, but plague was intermittent before that and struck London in 1603 when Herbert was living with his mother at Charing Cross. It struck again later, requiring him to shelter in his mother's house, then in Chelsea, for a year. Lancelot Andrewes, among other roles, was Vicar of St Giles Cripplegate, which had a population of 4,000 people at the beginning of 1603. By the end of the year, 2,878 of his parishioners had been killed by the disease.

## A man much blessed

Except for robust health, Herbert had everything going for him. First of all, at a time when most of the population were agricultural labourers, he was born into the wealthy upper elite. He belonged to the Norman Welsh aristocracy, with his family seat at Montgomery Castle, now in Powys but previously in the county town of Montgomeryshire. His wider family included the Earl of Pembroke in the south of Wales and the Earl of Carnarvon in the North. He was conscious of his family's distinction, and about the only criticism that Isaak Walton, the first biographer of Herbert, makes of him is that, as a student at Cambridge, it was said of him that 'he kept himself too much retired, and at too great a distance with all his inferiors; and his clothes seemed to prove that he put too great a value on his parts and parentage'.[2]

Second, although Herbert's father died when he was young, he had an intelligent, cultured and devout mother who safeguarded him to maturity. She was a remarkable woman in her own right, part of the literary circle at the time and especially a good friend of John Donne. She ensured that he had a good education, and Herbert came to share her serious faith.

Not least, Herbert was both highly talented and hard working. He did well at Westminster School, where he had a high reputation, went to Cambridge young, as was the custom in those days, and became a major Fellow of Trinity College at the age of twenty-three. His talents were not just academic. He was highly musical, playing the lute and the viol and singing his own compositions. He wrote poetry from an early age in both Latin and English.

## Herbert's formation

Herbert was born in Montgomery, not in the castle, which by then was a ruin, but in a large house, Blackhall, which his grandfather had built in the town. His father died when he was three, in 1596, so the following year his mother, Magdalene, moved in with her mother-in-law, Margaret Newton, at Eyton-upon-Severn, near Shrewsbury, a family much richer than the Herberts.

Only two years later Margaret Newton died, so in 1599 Magdalene and her family moved to Oxford to be near her eldest child, Edward, who was being educated there. As the eldest, and the heir, special attention would have been paid to his education, together with a motherly care that he did not fall into bad company at Oxford. It was an attention from which all the children benefited.

Two years later, in 1601, Magdalene moved to Charing Cross and in 1604 George started at Westminster School.

In 1609 Magdalene married Sir John Danvers, a wealthy and benevolent man who proved a generous stepfather to George. The family moved to his house in Chelsea.

Today we think of London as one vast conglomerate, but it is important to note that in Herbert's time there were a number of very distinctive communities separated from one another by a short distance. To the east was the City, the centre of commerce. To the west was Whitehall, the centre of court life, and further west, Westminster Abbey and the Houses of Parliament. Charing Cross was nicely pitched between them and Chelsea, where the family eventually went, again not too far from any of them. So Herbert was well placed to be in touch with all forms of elite life: financial, royal, political and religious. It was also a focus of literary life.

There was another feature of Herbert's formation that is worth noting. His grandfather had installed a long table at the house he built in the town of Blackhall and was known for his hospitality. After Herbert's father died and the family moved to Eyton-upon-Severn, again there was a reputation for lavish hospitality and bounty to the poor. Similarly, when the family moved to Charing Cross and later Chelsea, this was exercised on a generous scale.

## The glamour and glitter of success

At the age of seventeen, Herbert went to Cambridge as an undergraduate at Trinity College. Trinity is the grandest of the colleges, with a spacious quadrangle accessed via imposing gates. The Master of the college was a friend of his family and was supportive of the young student, who worked hard and prospered as an academic. By 1616 he was a full Fellow of Trinity and was soon asked to act on behalf of the university in various matters before, in 1620, being elected Public Orator. The role, then and now, is to give an address in honour of someone obtaining an honorary degree or in praise of some public dignitary. Then it was always in Latin, and often is now. This was no problem for Herbert, with his solid grounding at Westminster School. Indeed, his earliest poetry was in Latin.

In 1623 he delivered the farewell oration to James I and an oration to Prince Charles on their visits to the university. He had been noticed by James, who started to draw him into his court circle. Newmarket, where the King went for the races, was not far away.

All seemed set for George to prosper further. His elder brother had gone off to be Ambassador in Paris, and both his predecessors as Public Orator had likewise been appointed ambassadors. But Herbert was unsettled.

## The doldrums

In 1617 two of Herbert's elder brothers died, and the following year he wrote to his stepfather, Sir John Danvers, about 'setting foot into divinity'. That sounds very tentative, like putting a foot into the water, but clearly something was stirring. He may have been encouraged by the example of his great friend and hero Nicholas Ferrar, who had returned to England by then, and also by the learned and holy Lancelot Andrewes, whom Herbert might have met during this period. Although the standard of the clergy was rising at the time, as the numbers who studied at Oxford or Cambridge rose, their prestige was low and it was not a profession an able and ambitious young man would be expected to follow. But Ferrar and Andrewes were shining exceptions who would have encouraged Herbert.

In February 1622, only two years after taking up the position of Public Orator, Herbert became seriously ill and was said to be at 'death's door'. It was the beginning of an unsettled period in his life. With the support of a kinsman he became an MP, but does not seem to have made any impact or indeed attended Parliament much. During the period of the plague he stayed in his mother's house in Chelsea and then later with a friend in Kent. At the same time, he moved slowly towards a ministry in the Church. In 1624 he was ordained deacon and became co-portioner of a small parish in Montgomeryshire, and then a Prebendary of Lincoln Cathedral, which was linked to the parish of Leighton Ecclesia. He took this seriously, to the extent of raising a large sum of money, including from his own resources, to rebuild the dilapidated church to which his canonry was linked. Then, believing that a village parson should be married, he had the good luck to meet Jane, the favourite daughter of a relative of his father-in-law who had, according to Isaak Walton, long wanted her to marry George. They married three days after they were introduced. John Aubrey, a relative of Jane, wrote, 'His marriage, I suppose, hastened his death. My kinswoman was a handsome *bona roba* and ingenious.'[3] Aubrey translates *bona roba* as 'wanton'. A modern definition is 'an attractive woman who is sexually available', but for Aubrey at that time and in that context it would have meant 'lively' or 'sportive'. All the evidence suggests it was a very happy marriage.

Finally, at the age of thirty-six, he was ordained priest and took on the living of St Peter's, Fugglestone with Bemerton, not far from Salisbury.

## Purpose and peace

According to Walton, when George Herbert was inducted to the living of Bemerton, he went into the church alone for a period before tolling the bell. His friends outside waited some time, and when they looked through the window they saw him prostrate on the ground. This act of proskynesis, in which the person lies head down, flat on the floor, arms stretched sideways or forward, is made today by those about to be ordained priest and by some during the Good Friday Liturgy. It was at this time of total submission that Herbert vowed to keep the strict rule he had written for himself. His desire to give God all that he was, not just part of himself, found its fulfilment.

We see what this meant in practice in Isaak Walton's life of Herbert. Isaak Walton is best known as the author of *The Compleat*

*Angler*, but he also wrote about the lives of Anglican divines, including that of Herbert in 1670. Even more clearly, we see the reality in
*The Country Parson* by Herbert himself. Something of that ideal is
also set out in one of his less mature poems, 'Perirrhanterium', or
'The church-porch'. In thirty-seven chapters in *The Country Parson*, Herbert sets out what today we would call a combination of job
specification and professional code of conduct. The standard is high,
but one Walton believed Herbert fully met. Indeed, he felt it was a
life of such sanctity he was not up to describing it, but felt he must do
so, adding, 'I… profess myself amazed when I consider how few of
the clergy lived like him then and so many live so unlike him now.'[4]

This way of life meant first a strong personal discipline in his own
prayers and lifestyle. He knew well that his practice was going to be
much more eloquent than his preaching. Second, it meant bringing
his family into this holy way of life, and also, if possible, the whole
village. So twice a day, at 10 a.m. and 4 p.m., the bell rang and he, his
family and such villagers as could manage it gathered in the church
for morning and evening prayer.

He lived with a rhythm to his life that became, partly under his
influence, the ideal for the vast majority of parish clergy right up to
the Second World War. The morning would be spent reading. He
stressed the need for a good library of books, especially the church
fathers. The afternoons would be spent visiting those in need, the
sick and those who needed reconciling to their neighbours. George
and his wife Jane supported many of the destitute financially and the
whole parish pastorally. At that time the village parson was the welfare state. We see this even in the nineteenth century in the great wit
Sydney Smith, for example. Before Sydney Smith went to London, he
was vicar of a small parish in Yorkshire where he was in effect the
village doctor, the village pharmacist and the welfare officer. Herbert
would have offered the same whole-person ministry.

This was not, however, to the detriment of his spiritual ministry.
He took preaching very seriously and, after what he admitted was

a rather fulsome first sermon, he said he would keep his sermons simple and straightforward. He did this by concentrating on a teaching ministry, educating people in the meaning of the services and the Church's year and regular catechising.

Hospitality, in the tradition of his family, was an important part of his ministry, not just to those of his class but also to the whole parish.

It was not all severity. Although Herbert said there will always be an underlying sadness for a Christian because of the sin and suffering in the world and Christ's crucifixion, he realised that if there was only this it would put people off, so he allowed 'mirth'. He allowed himself to enjoy the rituals of village life, which brought people together and which he thought were important for communal life. His own personal pleasure, however, was music. Twice a week he walked to Salisbury to enjoy the choral services in the cathedral, and on his way home he joined some friends for music-making.

Sadly, this way of life only lasted three years, and he died of tuberculosis at the age of thirty-nine. Jane was a widow for six years after his death and then for another thirteen years after the death of her second husband. She never stopped extolling the virtues of the first one.

## Magdalene Herbert and John Donne

So often in the case of great men, they would not have been what they were without the decisive influence of the women in their lives, very often their mothers. This was certainly the case with George Herbert. His mother Magdalene was a remarkable woman. As we have already seen, she took very great care to ensure that he had the best education of the day, at the same time keeping him clear of harmful influences. But in addition to her role as a mother, she was an intelligent and cultured person in her own right who, when she was at Oxford, was very much part of the best academic and literary circles. It was there, when George was seven, that John Donne first met her. Donne was so struck by her that, according to Walton, he wrote his poem 'The autumnal' for her, including the lines:

> No spring nor summer beauty hath such grace
> As I have seen in one autumnal face.[5]

Then in 1610 Donne dedicated his Holy Sonnets to her, the first fruits of his turn from secular to religious verse. Later, in 1625, Donne sheltered in her house in Chelsea, together with George and Edward Herbert, when the plague was raging in London.

When Magdalene died, Donne was not able to preach at the service, but later did so at a commemoration for her in which for more than an hour he set out her qualities: her cheerfulness and wit, her hospitality and generosity, her integrity and faith. He had a great deal for which to thank her. For Donne, with his wife and seven children and no fixed employment, was so poor that, when a baby died, he said that, while it was one less mouth to feed, he could not afford a proper burial. At this time of his life Magdalene Herbert was a major benefactor, keeping him financially afloat. No wonder he wept as he preached about her. In case there were any rumours about the nature of their relationship, Walton wrote that though Donne was struck with 'the beauties of her body, and mind', yet it 'was not an amity that polluted their souls'.[6]

Together with her intellectual and spiritual qualities, Magdalene Herbert was physically attractive. In his funeral oration, Donne said that God gave her such 'comeliness' that she did not need to use make-up. She dressed modestly in clothes of good taste. Although in her last years when she was ill she suffered from depression, she did not complain about it.[7]

Certainly, Magdalene was comely enough to attract a second husband, who was said to be so handsome people came out to look at him[8] and was wealthy enough to marry any woman in the land. She married Sir John Danvers in 1609. He was half her age, the same age as her elder son Edward and only ten years older than George, who was then at Cambridge. Donne had a nice passage in his commemoration saying that their combined aged was sixty, so he would give them thirty years each:

> For, as the well tuning of an instrument, makes higher and lower strings, of one sound, so the inequality of their years was thus reduced to an evenness, that she had a cheerfulness, agreeable to his youth, and he had a sober staidness, conformable to her more years.[9]

John Aubrey put it more briefly: he married her for her 'wit' – her intellectual liveliness. John Donne wrote a poem expressing pleasure that they had married, and he remained friends with both of them.

As we have seen, Herbert was very blessed to have had such a mother. He was also blessed to have known in Donne a poet of such ability and a man who later in life turned that poetry towards God.

# Lancelot Andrewes, Nicholas Ferrar and Herbert's Church of England

The two great clerical role models for Herbert were Lancelot Andrewes and Nicholas Ferrar. Lancelot Andrewes was prodigiously learned, speaking fifteen modern and six ancient languages. He combined this with a deep piety, keeping his mornings free for prayer. At first a Canon, and then Dean of Westminster, which he became when Magdalene Herbert and her family moved to Charing Cross, he was a decisive influence on Westminster School and George Herbert himself. When Herbert was in a quandary about whether or not to be ordained, he made the long journey from Cambridge to Winchester, where Andrewes was bishop, to consult him.

One of the influences that first drew T. S. Eliot to the Christian faith was the literary quality of Andrewes's sermons, which he came to prefer to those of Donne. As Eliot put it:

Andrewes takes a word and derives the world out of it; squeezing and squeezing the word until it yields a full juice of meaning which we should never have supposed any word to possess.[10]

A superlative example of this is Andrewes's Good Friday sermon for 1604 on Lamentations 1:12, a key text for the day:

Have ye no regard, O all ye that pass by the way? Consider and behold, if ever there were sorrow like my sorrow, which was done unto me.[11]

Andrewes returns again and again to the notion that there is nothing comparable to such sorrow, non sicut.[12] The influence of this can be seen in Herbert's poem 'The sacrifice', with its repetition of the line, 'Was ever grief like mine?' (This poem is not included in this book but is suitable for Lenten reading.) More widely, the precision, concision and love of words that Andrewes cultivated at Westminster and which he took particular trouble to impart to the senior boys were very much part of Herbert, as was his personal piety.

Nicholas Ferrar's family was bound up with the Virginia Company in America. When this was taken over as a Royal Colony, Ferrar moved in 1626 with his family to Little Gidding, in a sparsely populated part of Huntingdonshire, where he purchased the manor and restored the church. He himself was ordained deacon so he could lead the community he had established there in a life of prayer. It was not a formal religious community and no vows were taken, but it sought to live out the Christian life in a communal way. He and Herbert had serious dealings with one another when Herbert was made a Canon of Lincoln Cathedral. As mentioned earlier, this was linked to the living of Leighton Bromswold, not far from Little Gidding, to which Herbert had to be instituted in person. When Herbert decided to rebuild the dilapidated church there, he entrusted the work to Ferrar, he himself concentrating on the fundraising. When Herbert was at Bemerton, following a similar way of life to the Little Gidding community, they continued to correspond. Finally, it was to Ferrar that Herbert sent his poems to decide whether they should be published or destroyed; to be published only if Ferrar felt they could be of use to other souls.

Charles I visited Little Gidding three times, taking refuge there during the Civil War. It was destroyed by Cromwell but came into prominence again as a result of the efforts of Eliot, among others, and the influence of what he wrote in 'Little Gidding', the last and greatest of his *Four Quartets.*

The church of George Herbert was clearly a church of the Reformation. It used the 1552 prayer book, which was more Calvinist than those of either 1549 or 1662, the one which is authorised up to our own day. At the same time, it retained a deep respect for the church fathers, believed in the application of human reason and was happy with a modest and restrained ceremonial. In the army there is a phrase about everything being correct and in good order. It is an ideal that very much accords with Herbert's temperament. He liked everything correct and in good order, the latter in two senses: both in good condition and ordered. We see this, for example, in the careful arrangement of *The Country Parson*, all the different aspects of the life carefully arranged under different headings. We see it in his poetry, the way he loved to order words according to different patterns. It is reflected in the way he thought the parson ought to order both the parish and his own household. It was reflected in his dress which, according to Isaak Walton, he always liked to be clean and neat. This is how he thought other clergy should be, and how the Church should look, following the injunction of Paul in 1 Corinthians 14 that everything should be done decently and in good order. He sought a middle way between 'superstition and slovenliness'.[13]

The Church Herbert served was the Church as described by the sixteenth-century divine Richard Hooker, who defined it as a *via media* between Rome and Geneva. As the priest/poet R. S. Thomas put it, for Herbert:

Anglicanism was a way of life. It was the commitment to an order of reason, discipline and propriety embodied in a Church solidly based on scripture and the Book of Common Prayer.[14]

# The great conflict

The picture we have of Herbert from his first biographer Isaak Walton and his friend Nicholas Ferrar, as well as from Herbert's own ideal as set out in *The Country Parson*, is of a saintly figure quietly leading his family and villagers in worship until his early death at the age of thirty-nine. That picture is not false, but it does not take into account what is so clearly apparent in the poetry: a person of strong emotions struggling with many inner conflicts. We tend to contrast the passionate John Donne with the quiet, ordered George Herbert. Donne, for example, begins Sonnet 14 with the words 'Batter my heart', and ends with fierce sexual imagery:

> for I,
> Except you enthrall me, never shall be free,
> Nor ever chaste, except you ravish me.

But George Herbert is no less passionate. As he wrote in 'Nature':

> Full of rebellion, I would die
> Or fight, or travel, or deny
> That thou has aught to do with me.

Herbert wrote a number of poems in which he pictures himself in a fight with God and as someone struggling to escape from an antagonist, of which the most powerful is 'The collar':

> I struck the board, and cry'd, No more;
> I will abroad.

As the poem continues, he 'raved and grew more fierce and wild'. The poems of George Herbert have to be seen in relation to that conflict and its partial resolutions; the apparently placid life of a country parson disguised a passionate man who had survived many intense emotional and spiritual conflicts. It is from these, allied to Herbert's musical sense and verbal artistry, that the poetry gets its strength.

Although the poetry of Herbert makes a strong appeal to believer and unbeliever alike, there is one theme among them that goes against the grain of modern sensibilities. He seems to be perpetually conscious of his sinfulness. In the modern world, where we are encouraged to think well of ourselves, we find this difficult to take. But taking it seriously for Herbert and trying to understand the reason for it is, I believe, the clue to getting inside the poet.

As the outline of his career makes clear, Herbert was ambitious, and in his earlier years he had hugely enjoyed the glamour and wit of fashionable life, in which he shone. After all, this was the milieu in which he belonged as a member of an aristocratic family and as someone who was cultivated and literary. Not least, he was a talented versifier who could write work that would be applauded by that circle.

Again, as discussed, Herbert's mother was deeply devout and brought up her children to follow her in this serious faith, which the young George did. He was not only clever and liked by others, but also pious. A letter written to his mother when he was seventeen, while studying at Cambridge, shows this clearly. He never turned away from that faith but he did get caught up in the world of glamour and worldly success. It was entirely in keeping with his talents that he should have been appointed Public Orator at Cambridge, responsible for making flattering and witty speeches in praise of visiting dignitaries. This he did with such success that a hugely successful career lay before him.

Then, his health, which was never robust, broke down and he was seriously ill. This was followed, in an age when everything depended on patronage, by the death of his two main patrons and, as Isaak Walton put it:

Not long after him King James died also, and with them, all Mr. Herbert's Court-hopes: so that he presently betook himself to a retreat from London, to a friend in Kent, where he lived very privately, and was such a lover of solitariness, as was judged to impair his health, more than his study had done. In this time of retirement, he had many conflicts with himself, whether he should return to the painted pleasures of a Court-life, or betake himself to a study of Divinity, and enter into Sacred Orders, to which his dear mother had often persuaded him. These were such conflicts, as they only can know, that have endured them; for ambitious desires, and the outward glory of this world, are not easily laid aside: but at last God inclined him to put on a resolution to serve at his altar.[15]

We need to take that passage with great seriousness. It is a story that is recounted in Herbert's poem 'The affliction (1)', which is discussed later.

Herbert was clear-eyed about what this would involve. No doubt because of his connections he would be able, if he wanted, to find a comfortable living, but, as he wrote:

The Country Parson knows well that both for the general ignominy which is cast upon the profession, and much more so for those rules which out of his choicest judgement he hath resolved to observe, and which are described in this book, he must be despised.[16]

This struggle about total commitment to God through ordination was the crisis in Herbert's life that is reflected one way or another in much of his poetry. There is a revealing passage in *The Country*

*Parson* when he is writing about the parson's library, in which are books about holy lives and where he finds wisdom about the nature of repentance:

> ... having for his own use examined the nature of it, is able to explain it after to others. And particularly having doubted sometimes whether his repentance were true, or at least in that degree that it ought to be, since he found himself sometimes to weep more for the loss of some temporal things than for offending God.[17]

He then goes to point out, as we would say, that some people are more outwardly emotional than others, or, as he puts it, 'as concerning weeping... some being of a more melting temper than others'. What matters is not what happens to the body, over which we have little control, for 'repentance is an act of the mind'.

That is eminently wise pastoral advice, but the point I want to take from this passage is the reference to weeping 'more for the loss of some temporal things than for offending God'. Here is a reference to the successful worldly career that had been taken from him and which he had sincerely renounced with his dramatic change of direction, but which from time to time still grabbed him emotionally with its attraction.

Do people only turn to religion when all else fails? Sadly, that is often the case. But those who do turn in that way often say that what failure brought home was the shallowness of their previous existence. Suffering, they say, put them in touch with the deeper grain of existence. They are glad of the failure. But this transition is unlikely to take place in a moment. It is an insight that has to be recaptured time and again, as old ambitions and regrets surface and have to be wrestled with once more. That process we see in the poems. To repeat the words of Walton:

These were such conflicts, as they only can know, that have endured them; for ambitious desires, and the outward glory of this world, are not easily laid aside.[18]

So Herbert, talented, witty and ambitious, very much part of a glamorous circle round the King, turns his back on that world to live as one who does not count in the world's eyes, as an unfashionable country parson. And the point about that turn as far as Herbert was concerned was that, at least at Bemerton, it was decisive, wholehearted, total, no reservations, no ifs or buts. But how could it be? Can we change like that in an instant? What was so distressing to Herbert was that, being self-aware, he found he had not totally changed in the way he wanted. This is why he blamed himself. We can therefore only understand this and appreciate it if we understand also the seriousness and total resolve of his turn away from worldly success to humble service. Only against that background can we appreciate the full strength of the poetry, not just its charm and musicality.

It is not possible to date the process in detail, as we do not know the dates of the poems. We do know, though, that Herbert was brought up in the piety of his mother and was a serious Christian. It was not a turn from unbelief to belief. But it was a decisive rejection of worldly ambition for a complete dedication to the service of God as an ordained minister. The first chapter of *The Country Parson* begins with the words, 'A pastor is the deputy of Christ, for the reducing of man to the obedience of God.' 'Reducing' is a strong, rather harsh word. The rest of the book makes clear that the first priority is that the priest has to reduce every aspect of his own life to the obedience of God. For Herbert, this was first of all his worldly ambition. Then it was lust.

In the chapter on 'The parson's state of life', he writes of the dangers of being single – which he was for most of his life. A single priest should not have a woman housekeeper or be alone with a woman or joke with them:

He keepeth his watch and ward, night and day against the proper and peculiar temptations of his state of Life, which are principally these two Spiritual pride, and Impurity of heart: against these ghostly enemies he girdeth up his loins, keeps the imagination from roving, puts on the whole Armour of God, and by the virtue of the shield of faith, he is not afraid of the pestilence that walketh in darkeness, [carnal impurity] nor of the sickness that destroyeth at noon day, [Ghostly pride and self-conceit.] Other temptations he hath, which, like mortal enemies, may sometimes disquiet him likewise; for the humane soul being bounded, and kept in, in her sensitive faculty, will run out more or less in her intellectual. Original concupiscence is such an active thing, by reason of continual inward, or outward temptations, that it is ever attempting, or doing one mischief or other. Ambition, or untimely desire of promotion to an higher state, or place, under colour of accommodation, or necessary provision, is a common temptation to men of any eminency, especially being single men.[19]

Herbert's poems are full of self-blame, and we can but presume that among the sins for which he blamed himself were the ones he thought were particularly dangerous to his calling: ambition, spiritual pride and lust. All that he felt and thought, all that he was, had to be brought into total submission to God. But that is a process, not a once-and-for-all act. We can see why if we start with the basic fact that we are born with a desire to live and thrive. There is nothing wrong with this in itself, for without it we would not live more than a few days. But we are called to grow beyond this to attend to others and their reality, especially the reality of God. This is a painful process, and when it occurs it is a kind of miracle, perhaps the greatest of all. This is what Herbert wanted, to be wholehearted, fully given over. So he ends 'The affliction (1)' with the line, 'Let me not love thee, if I love thee not.' In other words, unless he could love God with all his heart and soul and mind and strength, he would rather not love God at all.

What Herbert discovered in himself was how much growing there was still to do towards this great goal, how much he still hankered after the glamour of fashionable life, for example; how little he was in fact dedicated to God. In 'The sinner', for example, he looks in his heart to see if it is fully committed and:

> I finde there quarries of pil'd vanities,
>> But shreds of holinesse…
> In so much dregs the quintessence is small:
>> The spirit and good extract of my heart
>> Comes to about the many hundred part.

Herbert will have understood all this as sin, an aspect of original sin, the fallen state of humanity, together with the failures for which he was responsible. We might prefer to see it as an awareness of how far we have or have not travelled, how much or how little we have grown. What matters is the honest self-awareness. With this we can be more relaxed in our relationship with God, which in some of his poems, such as 'Discipline', Herbert is. God is a friend who can be chided. Every priest knows that there are still those who feel weighed down by feelings of inadequacy or self-blame. For such, these poems can be a balm, like the poet Coleridge, who said they helped him 'with his tendency to self-contempt'.[20]

One of the reasons Herbert's poems are so appealing is the way they go beyond feelings of self-blame to focus on the loving kindness of God. Mentions of hell in his poetry are conspicuous by their absence, there being only one. Particularly in the final poems there is an endearing picture of being accepted by God, however unworthy we might feel.

The other great issue for Herbert concerned his talent as a poet. How was this to be deployed? As early as seventeen he wrote to his mother to say that he wanted to write religious rather than secular verse. But the appeal of secular verse long had a hold on him. How lovely to have one's verse admired in fashionable circles! He still had his singular gifts as poet and musician. Music was easy, for music had long been deployed in the praise of God, and he did this with his lute and viol and voice. But poetry was associated with secular subjects, especially with human love. So Herbert turned verse forms associated with human love, such as the aubade, the morning song to the beloved, to God.

But there were trickier questions than this. Herbert had, and knew he had, great skill in different verse forms. Would it be appropriate to use his linguistic ingenuity in poetry directed towards the praise of God? Would it not be more appropriate simply to praise God in a straightforward, simple way? For he also strove after directness of speech, simplicity. As he put in 'A wreathe', 'Give me simplicity, that I may live.'

Herbert answers his own question with some subtlety. Yes, it is best to be simple, but in arriving at that answer he uses all his poetic skills! So in 'Jordan (1)', the highest achievement of all ingenuity and skill is simply to say, 'my God, my King'. In the end, Herbert rejoices not only in God but also in the fact that he can deploy this talent to the full in his service. He could 'relish versing' as much as he relishes smelling the dew and the rain, as he writes in 'The flower'. As John Drury puts it so beautifully, 'Wit, intellectual play to find truth, is one of Herbert's most endearing qualities.'[21]

# Themes

Herbert was immersed in Latin and Greek literature from an early age, so translating and writing poetry were part of him, although the earliest examples that have survived are the two sonnets he wrote to his mother in 1610 when he was at Cambridge. There are two collections of his poems, one perhaps put together in 1618 when he was at Cambridge, referred to as W, and the other, final collection, which he sent to his friend Nicholas Ferrar at Little Gidding just before his death. This contains poems that are not in W and a few changes and improvements on some of those that are. It is not possible to securely date the order in which they were written, though occasionally we can hazard a guess.

The poems use a great variety of forms, with their rhythms and tones subtly matching the themes. Some of them are highly ingenious and required great skill in their execution. Herbert clearly had a very good ear, a quality that T. S. Eliot particularly looked for in other poets and which he himself possessed.

The word 'Advent' means 'coming', and traditionally this four-week period in the Church's year, as reflected in the set readings, has been used to focus on the second coming of Christ, until the very end of the period, when it switches to the first coming in the Incarnation at Christmas. The image of the second coming gave rise to the other way of thinking of Advent, in terms of death, judgement, heaven and hell. However we think of it, Advent is a time of preparation, and the poems selected for this book have been loosely organised round four themes suitable for this, or indeed any other period of preparation: first how Christ comes to us to search and win our hearts, and second how he welcomes us. Third, there is our response to this, simply holding to the Christ who holds us; then finally, praise.

Walton clearly marvels at the heroic sanctity of Herbert at Bemerton, the seriousness of his own prayers and his responsibility for the growth in faith of both his own household and the parish. He describes in detail the routine of Herbert's day, the acts of charity and, as he says, it paints a picture very different from that of the average clergyman. Walton clearly finds himself at a loss for words when trying to describe the total commitment that Herbert made for the last four years of his life as a parish priest. This deep devotion is clearly evident in all the poems. Yet there is a continuing sense of wrestling and struggling to bring his whole self into the service of God. This has a number of aspects, giving rise to a range of images.

First, there is the idea of a great battle between the recalcitrant side of him and God, with the free use of military metaphors. This is a fight between an infinitely stronger opponent and a weaker one, so that in the end the former inevitably prevails. In 'The reprisal', he writes:

> Couldst thou not grief's sad conquests me allow,
> But in all vict'ries overthrow me?
> Yet by confession will I come
> Into the conquest. Though I can do nought
> Against thee, in thee will I overcome
> The man, who once against thee fought.

Second, this brings to the fore the ways in which the Divine will works to entice and draw the human soul, and here the images include impersonal as well as personal ones. Although Herbert was an opponent of extreme Calvinism and Puritanism, he was as firm as any in believing in the all-determining power of divine grace to win a human response. God is ceaselessly at work winning us over, at writing on our stone hearts, welcoming us.

At the same time there remains Herbert's acute self-awareness. In this painful self-knowledge he is very like T. S. Eliot, who thought we had to be restored by the refining fire of God's love, an image with which he ends 'Little Gidding'.

In 'Love (2)', Herbert writes on the same theme:

> Immortal Heat, O let thy greater flame
> Attract the lesser to it: let those fires,
> Which shall consume the world, first make it tame;
> And kindle in our hearts such true desires,
> As may consume our lusts, and make thee way.

This in turn leads Herbert, at least in some of his poems, to have a reposeful and confident trust, a peace of heart that he is in God's hands. This is brought out by poems that are sharply focused on the redemptive power of Christ's death, and more personally in those that are in dialogue form with the Divine. Here he could be quietly trusting like a child, as in 'Holy baptism (2)'.

Finally, this leads into the greatest of all of Herbert's themes. For him, human beings are made to appreciate, admire and go beyond this into ecstatic praise. Praise with all we are in every circumstance. He would have loved a later poet, Christopher Smart, who wrote, 'Praise above all – for praise prevails.'[22]

When I used these poems as the basis for a study group in the parish, one member remarked after a few weeks that, though he admired their skill, the themes did not speak to his condition. It was an important point to make. George Herbert's intense relationship with God and his strong sense that he was a sinner are not natural in our age. We encourage people to think well of themselves, not badly. But in studying Herbert, whose life was driven by an intense, passionate relationship with God, we may find a healthy corrective to some of our own concerns. Above all, it encourages self-knowledge and a greater awareness of our own heart, leading to a deeper peace and the possibility of praise.

Week 1

# WINNING THE HEART

# Monday
## The affliction (I)

When first thou didst entice to thee my heart,
    I thought the service brave;
So many joys I writ down for my part,
    Besides what I might have
Out of my stock of natural delights,
Augmented with thy gracious benefits.

I looked on thy furniture so fine,
    And made it fine to me;
Thy glorious household-stuff did me entwine,
    And 'tice me unto thee.
Such stars I counted mine: both heav'n and earth;
Paid me my wages in a world of mirth.

What pleasures could I want, whose King I serv'd,
    Where joys my fellows were?
Thus argu'd into hopes, my thoughts reserv'd
    No place for grief or fear.
Therefore my sudden soul caught at the place,
And made her youth and fierceness seek thy face.

At first thou gav'st me milk and sweetnesses;
    I had my wish and way;
My days were straw'd with flow'rs and happiness;
    There was no month but May.
But with my years sorrow did twist and grow,
And made a party unawares for woe.

My flesh began unto my soul in pain,
    'Sicknesses cleave my bones;
Consuming agues dwell in ev'ry vein,
    And tune my breath to groans.'
Sorrow was all my soul; I scarce believ'd,
Till grief did tell me roundly, that I liv'd.

When I got health, thou took'st away my life,
    And more, for my friends die;
My mirth and edge was lost, a blunted knife
    Was of more use than I.
Thus thin and lean without a fence or friend,
I was blown through with ev'ry storm and wind.

Whereas my birth and spirit rather took
    The way that takes the town;
Thou didst betray me to a ling'ring book,
    And wrap me in a gown.
I was entangled in the world of strife,
Before I had the power to change my life.

Yet, for I threaten'd oft the siege to raise,
    Not simp'ring all mine age,
Thou often didst with academic praise
    Melt and dissolve my rage.
I took thy sweet'ned pill, till I came where
I could not go away, nor persevere.

Yet lest perchance I should too happy be
    In my unhappiness,
Turning my purge to food, thou throwest me
    Into more sicknesses.
Thus doth thy power cross-bias me, not making

32

Thine own gift good, yet me from my ways taking.

Now I am here, what thou wilt do with me
    None of my books will show;
I read, and sigh, and wish I were a tree,
    For sure then I should grow
To fruit or shade: at least some bird would trust
Her household to me, and I should be just.

Yet, though thou troublest me, I must be meek;
    In weakness must be stout;
Well, I will change the service, and go seek
    Some other master out.
Ah my dear God! though I am clean forgot,
Let me not love thee, if I love thee not.

This is the most autobiographical of Herbert's poems. 'When first thou didst entice to thee my heart', it begins. The word 'entice', which reappears in the second verse as ''tice', is revealing. It suggests an attractive, gentle pull; something that lures or draws us. The one whom the poet addresses does not berate us but uses loving cunning to win us over. The enticement is enhanced by the fact that service in the rich mansion of God's presence at first allowed all the natural pleasures and delights of life to flourish. Service of God brought a world of pleasure, 'mirth' at that time meaning not so much laughter, as it does now, but sheer enjoyment. Service of God and taking pleasure in the good things of this life were not mutually exclusive. On the contrary, life seemed to get better in every way. During this time of perpetual May, no thought was given to 'grief or fear'.

Then came sudden sickness, physical pain which reduced the spirit to nothing. At the same time there were the deaths of loved members of the poet's own family, as mentioned in the introductory chapter, for the word 'friends' at the time could mean family as well as those whom we now think of as friends. The poet feels as helpless and useless as 'a blunted knife'. It forces him to do a rethink of his life. His aristocratic background and great talents made him a natural for the 'town', a life at court leading to some ambassadorship or Secretaryship of State. But he finds himself as an academic, involved in a world of disputation, and having to make flattering speeches in praise of visiting dignitaries. His spirit rebelled against it even if sometimes he was given 'the sweet'ned pill' of 'academic praise'.

He was stuck, entangled in this world before he had power to change his life. He could neither leave it nor persevere with it. The power that had given him 'milk and sweetnesses' at first seemed to have turned against him. The term 'cross-bias', which Herbert uses elsewhere as well, comes from the game of bowls. There was a bowling green at the house of his generous stepfather, Sir John Danvers, and also at his college, Trinity, in Cambridge. Bowls are designed with a bias so that they can curve in a particular direction, so to 'cross-bias' is to be deflected from one's proper course.

> Thus doth thy power cross-bias me, not making
> Thine own gift good, yet me from my ways taking.

In other words, he was not pursuing the way of life he had previously wanted, but nor was he finding any fulfilment in the way that God apparently wanted for him. None of his books showed him what to do and he was being totally unproductive and useless. Being useful and creative mattered to Herbert, and elsewhere also he complains when this is not happening. We might compare Gerard Manley Hopkins in his last terrible sonnets:

> See, banks and brakes
> Now, leavèd how thick! lacèd they are again
> With fretty chervil, look, and fresh wind shakes
> Them; birds build – but not I build; no, but strain,

Time's eunuch, and not breed one work that wakes.
Mine, O thou lord of life, send my roots rain.[1]

Herbert's poem comes to a remarkable conclusion in the final verse, in which the poet does two rapid about-turns. First, he suggests he must meekly and stoically accept what is happening to him. Then he rejects this and says he will reject the service of God altogether and seek another 'master', a favourite word of Herbert for God. But then he concludes:

Ah my dear God! though I am clean forgot,
Let me not love thee, if I love thee not.

The forgetting could be a complaint that God has forgotten him, but also the fact that in this rebellion he has forgotten both himself and the God who earlier gave him such happiness. The final line is a heartfelt cry that tells us so much about Herbert and serves to set his whole life and poetry in perspective. If he could not love God whole-heartedly, he did not want to love him at all. He wanted to be able to love him even in these dire straits. He wanted a love so authentic, so real, that it could cleave to God even in the worst afflictions of life.

If this poem had been written towards the end of his time at Cambridge but before he had fully committed himself to ordination, that last sentence well reflects the state of mind he was likely to be in at that time. Only later, when he lay prostrate on the floor of Bemerton, was he able to feel more confident that he was indeed wholehearted in his love.

This poem is mostly written in the most familiar form of English verse, the iambic pentameter with the second and fourth lines in trimeter which contains two syllables in each word, with the stress on the second one. It is the natural rhythm of walking and a natural way of recounting a life's journey, moving the reader along at an easy pace.

Everyone's spiritual journey is different. There may be times of feeling close to God (however few) and others when God seems absent. For everyone in life, there are good times and bad times, periods of real fulfilment and periods of frustration or depression. Like Herbert, we can reflect on that journey and try to understand it in terms of one who wants to entice not only our heart with the occasional good intention, but also our whole being.

# Tuesday
# The sinner

Lord, how I am all ague, when I seek
    What I have treasur'd in my memory!
    Since, if my soul make even with the week,
Each seventh note by right is due to thee.
I find there quarries of pil'd vanities,
    But shreds of holiness, that dare not venture
    To shew their face, since crosse to thy decrees:
There the circumference earth is, heav'n the centre.
In so much dregs the quintessence is small:
    The spirit and good extract of my heart
    Comes to about the many hundredth part.
Yet Lord restore thine image, hear my call:
    And though my hard heart scarce to thee can groan,
    Remember that thou once didst write on stone.

The introductory chapter discussed the reaction of many modern readers to those poems of George Herbert in which he accuses himself before God. In an age when people are encouraged to believe in themselves, Herbert's approach may well not be to our taste. Indeed, some modern writers on Herbert, including the best, have made clear their distaste for this. The traditional response to the modern criticism has been to say that the closer we come to God, the more aware we will be of how far short we fall of the love he shows to us and asks of us. But this answer is too general to convince. It needs to be grounded, and it is just this that Herbert gives us. As discussed in the introduction, at some point Herbert, always a believer, turned deadly serious in his relationship with God. Perhaps it was when he was made a deacon, or more likely when he was priested. Certainly, when he prostrated himself on the floor of Bemerton Church before his ordination, he felt himself to be fully dedicated. But we are never as fully dedicated as we would like to be and sometimes think ourselves to be. That is why it is essential to all true religion that there is some attempt at self-knowledge, some attempt to suss out the deceptions and evasions of our own heart.

In this sonnet the poet imagines himself looking back at the end of the day, as he recommends in 'Perirrhanterium', 'Sum at night what thou has done by day'. What he finds sickens him: 'I am all ague'. He knows from the story of creation, as reflected in the seven-day week, that at least one in seven parts of his time should be devoted to God. But what he finds are 'quarries of pil'd vanities' and only 'shreds of holiness'. In the outside world the earth is small compared to the surrounding sky, but inside himself the reverse is true, for heaven is dominated by earthly concerns. It is like liquid being distilled: 'the quintessence is small', only about a hundredth of what it began with. So the poet cries out to God to restore his image.

We human beings are made in the image of God (Genesis 1:27). We are able to think and choose, love and pray. But we have defaced that image. Christ himself is the true image, or icon: in him we see what a human being should be. He came among us that we might associate with him and have that image in us restored.

Herbert ends his poem referring to his hard heart but expressing the biblical hope that God can write on stone. This theme is taken up in the next poem.

The seriousness with which Herbert took his faith inevitably meant that he was aware not only of the reality of God, but also of his own heart. This awareness was sometimes painful, as it was for T. S. Eliot. In 'Little Gidding', the poet is told about the gifts reserved for age, especially the searing self-knowledge, when even what seemed good at the time came to seem self-serving.

When a friend, Conrad Aiken, bitterly criticised Eliot for his conversion to Christianity, Eliot replied:

> You may be right. Most of these criticisms I had anticipated, or made myself. Thrice armed is he who knows what a humbug he is. My progress, if I ever make any, will be purging myself of a large number of impure motives.[1]

So it was that, as 'Little Gidding' comes to a climax, the poet draws on a line from the fourteenth-century mystical writer Julian of Norwich to ask that our human motives might be purified in 'the ground of our beseeching'. Herbert and Eliot are very close here. Both are looking for complete pureness of heart.

# Wednesday
# Nature

Full of rebellion, I would die,
Or fight, or travel, or deny
That thou hast ought to do with me.
        O tame my heart;
    It is thy highest art
To captivate strong holds to thee.

If thou shalt let this venom lurk,
And in suggestions fume and work,
My soul will turn to bubbles straight,
        And thence by kind
    Vanish into a wind,
Making thy workmanship deceit.

O smooth my rugged heart, and there
Engrave thy rev'rend law and fear;
Or make a new one, since the old
        Is sapless grown,
    And a much fitter stone
To hide my dust, then thee to hold.

This is one of a number of poems in which Herbert expresses a sense
of rebellion against God, in which he and God are engaged in a life-
or-death struggle.

Herbert had high hopes for a successful secular career, then his
health, which was never robust, broke down and he was seriously ill. This was followed, in an age when everything depended on

patronage, by the death of his two main patrons. During the same period the call to ordination was growing more insistent and the result was a tug in his heart between two ways of life. God was calling, but was he ready to respond? Part of him reacted strongly against the idea of giving up the prospect of worldly success. As with John Donne, part of him rebelled. But his struggle had a different character from that of John Donne. In contrast to Donne's emphasis on God overthrowing him by sheer force, Herbert uses the image of taming. There is strength needed in taming an animal, but also shrewdness and kindness. Although both Donne and Herbert think in terms of a captured town or stronghold, Herbert uses the word 'captivate' with its sense of entice and enthral. And from God's side, this is not so much a war as an art, the 'highest art'.

In the second verse, the poet is aware not just of the weakness of his resolve but also of the poisonous character of some of his feelings. They are like a snake's venom. The lines suggest something like the witches' brew in Shakespeare's *Macbeth*, with its bubbles and fumes. But still in the last line there is a reminder that he is God's 'workmanship' (Ephesians 2:10 KJV). In some modern versions the Greek word is translated as 'work of art'.

The image of the heart, which occurs in the two previous poems, was hugely important to Herbert. In each of us there is a centre of thinking, feeling and choosing; a conscious 'I', an awareness that I am myself, thinking, feeling and choosing from one moment to the next. In the modern world we locate this in the brain, but in the biblical world it is referred to as the heart, and in the Hebrew Scriptures particularly it involves the whole person: body, mind and spirit. Sometimes in the New Testament, in the King James Version, the strong emotional side of this is referred to in terms of 'the bowels', as when Paul writes, 'For God is my record, how greatly I long after you in the bowels of Jesus Christ' (Philippians 1:8). In the Revised English Bible this becomes 'deep yearning'. For the most part, however, the image of the heart is the centre of all that makes me me. For

Herbert, religion is above all a religion of the heart. It involves his most intimate self and the relationship of that intimate self to the transcendent other. As he looks at his heart, he is aware that sometimes it is as cold, hard and unresponsive as a rock. So he prays that God may smooth the rugged rock of his hard heart and engrave it with his law. Or more than that, because it seems dead, 'sapless', it needs replacing by a new one altogether.

The last verse, and verses in a number of other poems also concerned with the heart and its hardness, draw on a number of references in the Bible. First, the story of God writing the Ten Commandments on stone (Exodus 31:18). Second, the plea that God can write, not just on stone but also on our hearts (2 Corinthians 3:3). Third, the fact that we need new hearts altogether (Jeremiah 31:31–3; Ezekiel 36:26).

In 'The altar', a short poem set at the beginning of his collection, Herbert asked that his heart be an altar:

A heart alone
Is such a stone,
As nothing but
Thy pow'r doth cut.

In another poem, 'Sepulchre', which picks up a number of different references to stone in the Bible, including the cold hard stone of the grave, Herbert again mentions our hard hearts, but ends on a note of hope, that nothing will stop God trying to win over humanity:

Yet do we still persist as we began,
And so should perish, but that nothing can,
Though it be cold, hard, foul, from loving man
    Withhold thee.

In Herbert's time, Calvinism, with its emphasis on God's irresistible grace, was a major stream within the Church of England. If Herbert was influenced by this, it was not as a hard dogma but as a personal hope. The love of God would never let him go, however hard his heart.

# Thursday
# The temper (I)

How should I praise thee, Lord! How should my rhymes
    Gladly engrave thy love in steel,
    If what my soul doth feel sometimes,
    My soul might ever feel!

Although there were some forty heav'ns, or more,
    Sometimes I peer above them all;
    Sometimes I hardly reach a score;
    Sometimes to hell I fall.

O rack me not to such a vast extent;
    Those distances belong to thee:
    The world's too little for thy tent,
    A grave too big for me.

Wilt thou meet arms with man, that thou dost stretch
    A crumb of dust from heav'n to hell?
    Will great God measure with a wretch?
    Shall he thy stature spell?

O let me, when thy roof my soul hath hid,
    O let me roost and nestle there:
    Then of a sinner thou art rid,
    And I of hope and fear.

Yet take thy way; for sure thy way is best:
    Stretch or contract me thy poor debtor:

This is but tuning of my breast,
To make the music better.

Whether I fly with angels, fall with dust,
Thy hands made both, and I am there;
Thy power and love, my love and trust,
Make one place ev'rywhere.

In modern parlance, this poem might be entitled 'Moods', as when we say of a person that they have a volatile temperament or a placid one. We all have different temperaments. Some people are subject to violent swings of emotion from ecstasy to depression; others are mildly depressive. But whatever our temperament, we will have swings from high to low, whether these be extreme or mild.

George Herbert was a man of intense emotion. He could not have been such a great poet without that capacity to feel deeply. He is not so obvious in his expression of those emotions as John Donne; he is less showy. But the intensity is there. In this poem he begins by noting how easy it would be to praise God in his poetry if he always felt as he did sometimes, on top of the world. But, as the next three verses indicate, he fluctuates in mood. Sometimes heaven seems close; sometimes hell. He feels racked or stretched. Here the image of God as the stronger one in a combat comes to the fore again. It seems unfair that God should 'meet arms', engage in armed combat, with tiny humanity.

In the first verse, the reference to 'steel' may bring to mind another context in which the word 'temper' is used. Steel is tempered, heated and cooled, stretched and compressed to the desired shape. This may be taken up again in the phrase 'meet arms', for when two combatants are duelling, they have to meet or measure their foils at the beginning.

This unfair combat is too much for the poet, so in verse 5 he expresses the desire to snuggle up into the roof of God and nest there free of all hopes and fears. It brings to mind Psalm 84:3 (KJV):

Yea, the sparrow hath found an house, and the swallow a nest for herself, where she may lay her young, even thine altars, o LORD of hosts.

Then, however, he reminds himself that God's way is best. There must be some purpose in all this stretching and contracting. Here another image comes to the fore. In those days, there were no tuning forks. Musicians had to test by ear, whether with a group or on their own, if their instrument was in tune. They had to stretch or contract the strings. This image is one that became increasingly important to Herbert and is explored more fully in the last section of this book: the idea of the human as a musical instrument that needs to be properly tuned. The good times and the bad times, the stretching and the contracting, work together to tune him for God's praise.

The poem comes to a fine end in the last verse. Whether the poet is feeling close to heaven or like just a piece of dust falling in the air, God is the ground of all being, angels and dust. In the last two lines there may be a deliberate alternative to John Donne. Donne had written a famous verse about two lovers resentful at being woken up by the sun: 'The sun rising'. They tell the sun that its work is done merely by shining on them: 'Shine here to us and thou art everywhere.' In another poem, 'The good-morrow', Donne wrote:

For love, all love of other sights controls
and makes one little room an everywhere.

Herbert, in contrast, addresses the divine love:

Thy power and love, my love and trust,
Make one place ev'rywhere.

In the divine love and its reciprocating human response, heaven and earth, God and humanity, are united. This is all that matters.

46

Wherever we are, or in whatever frame of mind, this union is present.

Our feelings matter; they are very much part of us, and we are right to be aware of them and to take them into account in our relationship with God. But it is important not to confuse our feelings with whether God is close or distant from us. For someone who is religious, swings of mood will often be closely allied with whether we are feeling close to or distant from God. If things are going well with us and we are feeling healthy on a sunny day, it might feel easy to offer God a prayer of praise. If we are going through a bad patch in our life, have had an uneasy night and are not feeling too good anyway, we might very well be feeling that God is absent from us. But it is important not to confuse the feeling with the reality. The Christian reality is that God is with us all the time, and indeed may be more intensely present in what we experience as darkness. Our emotions are not to be despised, and they are to be treated with due seriousness. Like Herbert, we can bring them into our prayers, but they are not a sure guide to the presence of God. Even when we are feeling down, a simple act of trust in God lifts us into a dimension that transcends time and space.

# Friday
# Discipline

Throw away thy rod,
Throw away thy wrath:
   O my God,
Take the gentle path.

For my heart's desire
Unto thine is bent:
   I aspire
To a full consent.

Not a word or look
I affect to own,
   But by book,
And thy book alone.

Though I fail, I weep:
Though I halt in pace,
   Yet I creep
To the throne of grace.

Then let wrath remove;
Love will do the deed:
   For with love
Stony hearts will bleed.

Love is swift of foot;
Love's a man of war,

And can shoot,
And can hit from far.

Who can 'scape his bow?
That which wrought on thee,
   Brought thee low,
Needs must work on me.

Throw away thy rod;
Though man frailties hath,
   Thou art God:
Throw away thy wrath.

This apparently simple and straightforward poem is remarkably revealing of Herbert at a particular stage in his life. What we notice about it is its tone. The poem addresses God and tells him what to do. It is a dangerous strategy, for it would be all too easy to sound presumptuous and inappropriate. This poem avoids that. Somehow the poet is able to address God in a way that is familiar, almost cheeky, yet at the same time to convey that this is an act of faith, not hubris.

Discipline is not an idea or a word that we find attractive. But discipline was very much part of the world in which Herbert lived, and indeed in which all human beings lived until the great cultural changes that took place in the Western world in the 1960s. Discipline is also part of the biblical world. In the Hebrew Scriptures, God is continually disciplining his people, either punishing them for wrongdoing or training them for faithful service. Herbert accepts that biblical world view but at the same time appeals to the other side of God. So he begins by telling God to throw away his rod and wrath and express the gentle side of his nature.

A feature of a good number of Herbert's poems is his self-blame, the way he is conscious of falling short of what he thinks God wants of him. In the next two verses, however, in strong contrast to this, he affirms what he finds in himself, his aspiration to fully submit to God and to live not by what he wants but by God's word in the Bible alone. Instead of accusing himself, he recognises and draws attention to the fact that there is something genuine and genuinely good in himself. But this does not come across like the boast of the Pharisee in the parable who thanked God he was not like sinners (Luke 18:11). It sounds what it is, a piece of honest self-recognition. There was good in him, and he was glad to see it.

This poem is not in *W*, the earlier text, so it reflects a mood in the last years of Herbert's life, when he knows he is as fully committed as he can be to the one he calls 'Master'. So he draws God's attention to this wholehearted commitment. Instead of castigating himself for falling short, he draws attention to his real desire to love God with his whole being. Though he knows he fails, he also knows that when he does so he is sincerely sorry and seeks God's grace. This, too, God should notice, as verse 4 points out.

So Herbert tells God to remove his anger because love will do all that is necessary. Love can melt the stoniest heart (verse 5) and love can touch him from anywhere, as verse 6 suggests. Exodus 15:3 says that 'The LORD is a man of war' (KJV). It has also been suggested that behind this image is a picture of Cupid with his bow firing darts of love. That is problematic because Herbert at the age of seventeen, in his first recorded sonnet, written to his mother, argues for the superiority of religious over secular verse, using the image of Cupid:

Cannot thy love
Heighten a spirit to sound out thy praise
As well as any she? Cannot thy Dove
Outstrip their Cupid easily in flight?

We know that no one is outside the reach of this love because it went to the length of Incarnation and death on the cross to gather us to itself. A love that was brought that low is no less at work in him (verse 7).

Then, in the final verse, sandwiched between the two commands that have run through the poem, that God throw away his rod and wrath, the poet acknowledges that human beings are frail (a less condemnatory word than 'sinner') and simply appeals to God as God: 'Thou art God.'

The reason that Herbert can write this poem telling God what to do in a way that does not jar is because implicit all the way through is a simple confidence that God is God, and God is a God of love who desires only human well-being. The tone is not presumptuous or peevish but one of friendly trust. It brings to mind the words of Jesus when he called his followers 'friends'. God is not only God, but he is also close to us as friend.

The form of this poem is unusual, and it is one that perfectly captures the tone of the message. Each verse contains three lines each with three feet, with the syllables alternating stressed and unstressed. The third line, however, consists only of three equal syllables. In good poetry, theme and form are perfectly fitted to one another, as they are here. It manages to sound friendly, matter of fact, to the point.

In creation, God says, 'Let there be...' He gives every aspect of creation a life of its own, which is what it means to be created. There has been a tendency in Christian history to think that everything that happens, good and bad, is directly willed by God, and in so far as they impinge on us, such things are to be seen in terms of a punishment, testing or training. For many people today, that is not a helpful way of seeing life. Better to accept that, in modern parlance, 'stuff happens', sometimes all too sad and tragic stuff. The mystery of why God allows particular events to happen remains. The Christian task is to align ourselves with Christ in trying to draw some good out of them. In doing this, Herbert encourages us to address God with all the confidence of an intimate, as someone able to be honest and real.

# Saturday

# Prayer (I)

Prayer the Church's banquet, angels' age,
    God's breath in man returning to his birth,
    The soul in paraphrase, heart in pilgrimage,
The Christian plummet sounding heav'n and earth
Engine against th' Almighty, sinners' tower,
    Reversed thunder, Christ-side-piercing spear,
    The six-days world transposing in an hour,
A kind of tune, which all things hear and fear;
Softness, and peace, and joy, and love, and bliss,
    Exalted Manna, gladness of the best,
    Heaven in ordinary, man well drest,
The milky way, the bird of Paradise,
    Church-bells beyond the stars heard, the soul's blood,
    The land of spices; something understood.

This is one of Herbert's finest poems, as all critics agree. Although it is in traditional sonnet form, it is also very modern, indeed modernist. This is because, instead of taking just one metaphor and developing it in different ways, it uses a series of very different images, twenty-six in all, to create and convey a particular emotional effect. Overall, this effect might be described as a combination of intimacy and elusiveness, of spiritual closeness and tantalising otherness. The use of images in this way, imagist poetry, was a feature of the modernism that emerged before the First World War, and of which T. S. Eliot made use in his own poetry.

It is also a poem that is strongly sensual, using especially the senses of sight, hearing and taste. In other poems, Herbert makes full use of the sense of smell, for example in 'The odour'. For him, the sensual and the spiritual combine happily in prayer.

The picture of the kingdom of God as a banquet is a familiar one in the parables of Jesus, and the phrase 'heavenly banquet' is part of Christian tradition. The Eucharist, which meant so much to Herbert, is a foretaste of that banquet. So too, in this poem, is prayer. In that banquet we are lifted beyond ourselves into another order, one in which the angels have their timeless existence.

In the Book of Genesis we read, 'Then the LORD God formed man from the dust of the ground, and breathed into his nostrils the breath of life; and the man became a living being' (Genesis 2:7). At death, this breath, this life-giving spirit, returns to God its origin. So Jesus when he died prayed, 'Father, into your hands I commend my spirit' (Luke 23:46). The title of a poem by Gerard Manley Hopkins states the idea beautifully: 'Thee, God, I come from, to thee I go'.

In prayer, our deepest feelings and most serious thoughts are expressed. Here, what is most important to us comes to the fore and is expressed in a few words. Here, our soul is in paraphrase, but this is not where we are to rest and stay. In prayer, we are on the move, on a journey. The heart is in pilgrimage.

As a ship sails close to the harbour, one of the sailors might put down a plumb line to find out how deep the water is. So in prayer, the Christian sounds the depths of heaven. In prayer, heaven and earth come close.

A number of Herbert's poems depict the idea of a struggle, a combat going on between God and the poet. Here, too, are images from the battleground. The engine was a device for hurling large stones into a city or to break down its walls. The tower gave height for shooting into the besieged city and also enabled its walls to be scaled. So prayer enables the Christian to break into God. This is 'reversed thunder' in that instead of rumbling on earth, our prayer rumbles and disturbs heaven. At the same time, it is a spear that pierces Christ's side. In the Gospels, that was an act of human aggression.

53

But in Christian tradition it became an image of entering into the heart of Jesus, and in John's Gospel the wound gives out both water and blood, the gift of the spirit and the blood of Christ shed for our salvation, sacramentally made present in the wine of the Eucharist (John 19:34).

A musical tune can be transposed into another key. So Herbert suggests that the six-day workaday world can be transposed in an hour of prayer into something even more musically pleasing. Indeed, prayer itself is 'a kind of tune' which fills the universe. It brings to mind the island in Shakespeare's *The Tempest*, in which we read:

Be not afeard, the isle is full of noises,
Sounds, and sweet airs, that give delight and hurt not.[1]

This prayer can be sheer bliss, even better than the manna by which the people of Israel were fed in the wilderness. The mood in these lines is one of ecstatic gladness.

'Heaven in ordinary, man well drest' is a vivid, down-to-earth image of the way God and humanity come together in prayer; God in jeans, as it were, humanity in a good suit. In the Incarnation, God meets us as we are. In Herbert's time, 'ordinary' was apparently a word used for an everyday meal. God comes to us in that accessible, everyday way. At the same time, prayer brings out the best in us.

The images in the last three lines bring out the tantalising, out-of-reach quality of some of our experiences. Many people are conscious of this in experiences of beauty. A beautiful scene in nature or a beautiful action by someone can move us deeply and at the same time leave a sense that there is something here we can never possess. Herbert experiences this in prayer. There is something there that is as mysterious and beyond us as the Milky Way, and as exotically beautiful as a bird of paradise, specimens of which were first brought back from the East Indies in the preceding century. Similarly, 'the land of spices' was distant and exotic, and the spices, which had been brought to Europe from the fifteenth century, valuable.

Most people find the sound of church bells, perhaps especially when they carry across the countryside from a distant church tower, haunting. They come to us from a mysterious distance but call us to be close. They summon us into some ultimate mystery. In prayer, they come from beyond the stars, stirring the soul's blood.

In the end there is simply 'something understood'. No more need be said, or indeed can be said. But that is a place of rest.

Week 2

# WELCOME

# Monday
# Love (3)

Love bade me welcome; yet my soul drew back,
    Guilty of dust and sin.
But quick-eyed Love, observing me grow slack
    From my first entrance in,
Drew nearer to me, sweetly questioning
    If I lack'd anything.

'A guest,' I answer'd, 'worthy to be here:'
    Love said, 'You shall be he.'
'I, the unkind, ungrateful? Ah, my dear,
    I cannot look on Thee.'
Love took my hand and smiling did reply,
    'Who made the eyes but I?'

'Truth, Lord; but I have marr'd them: let my shame
    Go where it doth deserve.'
'And know you not,' says Love, 'Who bore the blame?'
    'My dear, then I will serve.'
'You must sit down,' says Love, 'and taste my meat.'
    So I did sit and eat.

As we know, George Herbert grew up in a family characterised
by hospitality, most immediately as offered by his mother and his
stepfather Sir John Danvers, and before them by his grandparents.
Furthermore, as his was one of the most distinguished families in
the land, hospitality would have been expected as part of their way
of life.

In this poem, Love is the host. While at that time this would usually have been a man, at least during the time of her widowhood it would have been Herbert's mother, so the Love who welcomes us could be male or female. We can imagine him/her coming to the entrance of the room and simply saying, 'Welcome.' But the poet demurs. He loves cleanliness and he feels the dust of the journey on him, and not just physical dust but also the dust of human frailty, for when Adam sinned he was told, 'You are dust, and to dust you shall return' (Genesis 3:19). These words are used in the Book of Common Prayer burial service and in modern-day services of ashing on Ash Wednesday.

However, Love, in contrast to most of us who can too easily be absorbed in our own thoughts, has her eye focused on the guest. In a lovely phrase, 'quick-eyed Love' notices his hesitation, draws near and very gently asks if there is a problem.

The poem continues in its dialogue form, hesitation by the guest followed by reassurance from the host. The guest is assured that he is indeed the one who is expected and wanted. And when the guest still feels unworthy, so unworthy that he looks down, Love comes even closer, holds the poet's hand and smiles. The creator host is the one who has made those eyes that dare not look up, and he would not have done this unless she wanted him to join others at the table.

The guest is now in danger of becoming tedious with his expressions of unworthiness, so he is assured that, if there is any blame, it has already been borne by the host. Then we come to line 16, 'My dear, then I will serve', about which there is some argument. Some learned interpreters take this as another statement of the host, saying that not only has she taken the blame, but she will also serve at table, as Jesus did: 'I am among you as one who serves' (Luke 22:27). Though this breaks the sequence of a statement by the host followed by one from the guest in having three statements by the host in quick succession, Herbert did on occasion vary his fundamental pattern to create a new effect. However, I believe it makes more sense to take this as a statement of the guest. The guest accepts the invitation to come into the dining room, but he will do so only in order to serve the other guests rather than sit at table himself. But the host is adamant, he must sit at table as a guest. So finally, 'I did sit and eat.' All is resolved. There is nothing more needed or to be asked for, for what greater happiness is there than to sit at table in the company of family or friends with Divine Love presiding over all and imbuing all with loving laughter?

Herbert believed this was his finest poem, and one that summed up more than any other his deepest convictions. For this reason, both in the early version of his poems, W, and the final one, it comes last, followed by the word 'Finis'. Hugely admired in the past, it continues to be so today.

There is a wonderful sense of moving forward in this poem, from the first warm welcome to drawing near, holding hands and smiling. And this movement is reflected in each of the dialogues, with the opening words from Love being brisk and the answering slow and heavy; Love continuing to reach out and take the initiative, despite every drawing back of the guest.

The remarkable French intellectual, Simone Weil, of Jewish agnostic background, who suffered from crippling migraines, spent ten days at the monastery in Solesmes at Easter 1938. There, a young English Catholic recommended the seventeenth-century metaphysical poets, among them this poem, of which she wrote:

I learnt it by heart. Often, at the culminating point of a violent headache, I make myself say it over, concentrating all my attention upon it and clinging with all my soul to the tenderness it enshrines. I used to think I was merely reciting it as a beautiful poem, but without my knowing it the recitation had the virtue of a prayer. It was during one of these recitations that, as I told you, Christ himself came down and took possession of me.[1]

She had never prayed before, she had not read any of the mystics and she was put off religion by stories of miracles and divine apparitions, but she continued:

> Moreover, in this sudden possession of me by Christ, neither my senses nor my imagination played any part; I only felt in the midst of my suffering the presence of a love, like that which one can read in the smile of a beloved face.[2]

If I were told I had one last day on earth and was given the choice how to spend it, I would ensure it contained a meal with family or friends or both. If it were a sunny day, then it might be a picnic. W. H. Auden, in his poem 'Horae Canonicae', envisages the life to come as a picnic: we won't have anything to hide and we will all join in the dance. For what higher mortal state is there but a shared meal with those you are fond of? That is what rich or poor enjoy most, as long as love is there.

> Better is a dinner of vegetables where love is
> than a fatted ox and hatred with it.
> (Proverbs 15:17)

It is not surprising, therefore, that one of the pictures of the afterlife in the Bible is a heavenly banquet, or that Jesus in his teaching should so often use the image of a feast to describe some aspect of the kingdom of God. Nor is it surprising that the main Christian service, the Eucharist, should be thought of as a foretaste of that heavenly banquet. The service of Holy Communion, as he called it, meant much to Herbert and he wrote two poems with that title, though he only included one of them in the final version of his poems. In *The Country Parson*, he writes about the manner of receiving Communion: 'The feast indeed requires sitting, because it is a feast; but man's unpreparedness asks kneeling', but then he adds, 'contentiousness in a feast of charity is more scandal than any posture'. Herbert's poem is indeed a feast of charity.[3]

For Herbert, the divine generosity of the Eucharist was to be lived out in the hospitality of his household. So, again in *The Country Parson*, he writes:

> Now, love is his business and aim; wherefore he likes well that his parish at good times invite one another to their houses, and he urgeth them to it; and sometimes, where he knows there has been, or is, a little difference, he takes one of the parties, and goes with him to the other, and all dine or sup together. There is much preaching in the friendliness.[4]

# Tuesday

# Redemption

Having been tenant long to a rich lord,
    Not thriving, I resolved to be bold,
    And make a suit unto him, to afford
A new small-rented lease, and cancel th' old.
In heaven at his manor I him sought;
    They told me there that he was lately gone
    About some land, which he had dearly bought
Long since on earth, to take possession.
I straight returned, and knowing his great birth,
    Sought him accordingly in great resorts;
    In cities, theatres, gardens, parks, and courts;
At length I heard a ragged noise and mirth
    Of thieves and murderers; there I him espied,
    Who straight, *Your suit is granted*, said, and died.

This poem is one of Herbert's most masterly, the abrupt end leaving the
reader with a sense of astonishment. Unlike most of Herbert's poems,
which have a strong confessional element, this one is quite objective. It is not
about what the poet is feeling or thinking, but simply tells a story. In some
ways it is like the parables told by Jesus. For it is a story about everyday life
with a deeper meaning, and one which at the end poses a challenge to the
hearer or listener about where they stand in relation to that deeper meaning.

The poem, in sonnet form, appeared in *W* and then in the final
version with one change. The lines:

Sought him accordingly in great resorts;
In cities, theatres, gardens, parks, and courts;

originally appeared as:

> Sought him in cities, theatres, resorts,
> In grottoes, gardens, palaces and courts

which is much less musical. Herbert also changed the title from 'Passion' to the less explicit 'Redemption', for he liked his poetry to be suggestive rather than dogmatic. Also, the word 'redemption' has legal overtones, sometimes connected to land, which fits the imagery. A piece of land might have run up debts and then been redeemed when those debts were paid off.

The scene would have been all too familiar to people in the early seventeenth century. Most land was in the hands of big landowners. The majority of the population were agricultural labourers. But there was also a significant minority who were tenant farmers. Some had only a few acres, some much more, but all were characterised by being totally in the power of the rich lord, who had the power to evict or change the rent. One tenant who was 'not thriving', perhaps because the land was poor, resolved to plead with the landowner for a lease on a different farm that he could make pay. Not finding the lord at his manor house, he searched for him where the rich and powerful were usually to be found. Then he heard the sound of a street brawl or pub fight and found the lord on the point of dying, 'Who straight, *Your suit is granted*, said, and died.'

There are clues in the story to its deeper meaning. First, the lord had gone not just to buy any old land but one on 'earth' and one 'which he had dearly bought long since'. It brings to mind Revelation 13:8, with its reference to 'the Lamb who was slain from the creation of the world' (NIV). Then the fact that the lord was not to be found among the wealthy has as background the early Christian hymn in Philippians 2:6–8, in which Christ:

who, though he was in the form of God,
   did not regard equality with God
   as something to be exploited,
but emptied himself,
   taking the form of a slave,
   being born in human likeness.
And being found in human form,
   he humbled himself
   and became obedient to the point of death –
   even death on a cross.

Then, of course, the reference to 'thieves and murderers' is a vivid reminder that Christ was crucified between two criminals.

The tenant farmer sought a new farm because he was 'not thriving', and he wanted the old lease cancelled. It has been suggested that we have here a reference to the new realm of grace replacing the old realm of the law, which was so central to the apostle Paul's understanding of the Christian faith. But the 'not thriving' may go wider than that to refer to our whole human nature. In the end, the suit that is granted is our new nature, which in Christ can indeed thrive and flourish.

How does the death of the rich lord bring this about? Over time, the Church has come up with a number of different pictures in answer to that question, and part of the power of the poem is that it leaves the reader to ponder it themselves. Whatever answer we may come up with, the astonishing fact is that the Eternal Son of God came all the way to meet us, even when it meant meeting human hostility.

R. S. Thomas, the Welsh priest and poet, wrote an introduction to a selection of Herbert's poems. I think he must have been influenced by this poem in the writing of his own poem 'The coming'. This pictures God showing the Son a globe, and they peer at it until they see a figure on a cross. 'Let me go there, he said.'[1]

# Wednesday
# The call

Come, my Way, my Truth, my Life:
Such a Way, as gives us breath:
Such a Truth, as ends all strife:
Such a Life, as killeth death.

Come, my Light, my Feast, my Strength:
Such a Light, as shows a feast:
Such a Feast, as mends in length:
Such a Strength, as makes his guest.

Come, my Joy, my Love, my Heart:
Such a Joy, as none can move:
Such a Love, as none can part:
Such a Heart, as joys in love.

We have seen that many of Herbert's poems reflect an intense inner struggle. This one is quite different. It conveys a serene confidence – indeed, happiness – with all tensions, at least for the time being, resolved. It is at once simple and highly crafted, expressing strong religious feelings that are focused away from the poet himself and on Christ. Nearly all Herbert's poetry is characterised by a musicality, but none more so than this poem, and it is easy to understand why Ralph Vaughan Williams set it to music as one of his 'Five mystical songs', each based on one of Herbert's poems. The rhythm is a strong beat followed by a short one (a trochee) in each line with no final short, which breaks up any possible monotony.

For some people, the title of this poem, 'The call', first brings to mind God's call to us. But in fact the poem is a response by the poet, a call from the believer to Christ. Perhaps he has in mind Revelation 22:20, 'Come, Lord Jesus!'

Rupert Brooke wrote a poem called 'The great lover', in which he set out all the everyday things he loved, as did Elizabeth Jennings in her poem 'Praises' (which is also the name of the collection of poems in which that poem appears). Here, Herbert sets down all the aspects of God he loves. Others at the time wrote love songs about their human beloved, praising their different features and qualities. Herbert writes a love song for God about God.

From the first, we note that this is a God whom Herbert wants, not one who is imposed or accepted reluctantly. It begins, 'Come', and this is the first word of each of the three verses. Then we note, also in the first line, that the one he is calling is acknowledged and owned in the most intense and personal way possible. Three times the word 'my' is repeated, as again it is in the first line of the two succeeding verses.

The nouns in the first line come directly from the words of Jesus as reported in John 14:6. In the following three lines each one is made the object of an activity. The three characteristics are not just abstract truths; they affect the real world. The Way gives us breath for the journey, the breath that God breathed into humanity in the first place (Genesis 2:7) and the breath that Jesus breathed on his disciples to give them the Holy Spirit in John 20:22. The Truth is not just intellectual; it ends the cruel quarrels of humanity. Then, as a great climax, the Life that is given 'killeth death'. In a funeral service, as the coffin comes up the aisle, the priest proclaims (John 11:25–6):

I am the resurrection and the life, saith the Lord: he that believeth in me, though he were dead, yet shall he live: And whosoever liveth and believeth in me shall never die.[1]

The life of Christ lives in us now, a life that does not end with death.

In the second verse, the dominant image is that of a feast, the heavenly banquet of which the Eucharist is a pledge and foretaste and about which Herbert wrote so memorably in 'Love (3)'. It had earthly reality for Herbert, of course, in the tradition of hospitality in his family. 'I am the light of the world,' said Christ (John 8:12). This intellectual and spiritual light shows us both the feast ahead and life itself as a feast to which moment by moment God invites us. This is a feast that gets better the longer it goes on ('mends in length'), and at which it is possible for humans to be guests because the host not only issues the invitation but also provides the grace that enables us to accept and sit at table.

The process of internalisation in the first two verses becomes even more intense in the third. It concerns three emotions, though they are not only emotions. Joy and love are integrally related, as in the words of Jesus (John 15:10–12):

> If you keep my commandments, you will abide in my love, just as I have kept my Father's commandments and abide in his love. I have said these things to you so that my joy may be in you, and that your joy may be complete.
>
> This is my commandment, that you love one another as I have loved you.

This is a joy that nothing can remove and from which nothing can part us. It is the joy and love that characterise the heart, our centre of identity, the self that thinks and chooses and feels. This final line ties up the whole poem in a wonderful manner. For whereas all the lines before were moving forward, doing something to achieve some end, in the final line we have the end itself. It is a heart that rejoices in love. The order of the nouns in the first line of the third verse is reversed to bring about, 'Such a Heart, as joys in love'. What this line brings to mind is an everlasting circle, an image of eternity – for there is no further end beyond this. This is the goal, what all is designed to achieve.

We can see the reason why this is the goal when we reflect on the nature of happiness. Many human beings would say that they have known at least some moments or periods of happiness. At the same time, life is shot through with pain and anguish. Even if we are not experiencing it ourselves, we are aware of it daily through the news. So someone who is sensitive can never quite forget, even in periods of happiness and contentment, that there is a world of misery out there. So how, then, can there ever be a true happiness, one that nothing can remove? The last line tells us: it lies in rejoicing in the reality of love and seeking to live out that love in our relationships with others. This takes us into a dimension beyond the ordinary categories of sadness and happiness. It does not obliterate them. They remain; indeed, they may be felt even more acutely. But they are lifted into a realm of love which can be lived in both good and bad times.

# Thursday
# The twenty-third psalm

The God of love my shepherd is,
    And he that doth me feed:
While he is mine, and I am his,
    What can I want or need?

He leads me to the tender grass,
    Where I both feed and rest;
Then to the streams that gently passe:
    In both I have the best.

Or if I stray, he doth convert
    And bring my mind in frame:
And all this not for my desert,
    But for his holy name.

Yea, in death's shady black abode
    Well may I walk, not fear:
For thou art with me; and thy rod
    To guide, thy staff to bear.

Nay, thou dost make me sit and dine,
    Ev'n in my enemies sight:
My head with oil, my cup with wine
    Runs over day and night.

Surely thy sweet and wondrous love
    Shall measure all my days;

And as it never shall remove,
  So neither shall my praise.

Psalm 23 is the best known and best loved of all the psalms. In Herbert's time there were already a number of versions in English. There was the one in the King James Bible of 1611, the Authorised Version as it became known. There was also the one that had been written by Myles Coverdale, who produced the first authorised English version of the whole Bible, The Great Bible, in 1535 and which came to be included in the Book of Common Prayer. For ease of reference, this version is printed below. A metrical version was written by Sternhold and Hopkins in 1562, and the poet Philip Sidney, who influenced Herbert in various ways, also wrote a version. Later there have been other fine renderings, including the best known of all, the Scottish metrical version to the tune of Crimond.

But Herbert's poem, now sung as a hymn, has its own special quality. Herbert's version has six verses, each of four lines, a four-stress line being followed by a three-stress one. The first and third lines rhyme, as do the second and fourth.

Herbert begins with a resounding affirmation. The one he is extolling is 'The God of love', not just 'The Lord'. Then he expands the Book of Common Prayer's 'therefore can I lack nothing' in a delightful way, affirming a mutual belonging and ending almost with a shrug of his shoulders, so 'What can I want or need?'

Again, the second verse in the Book of Common Prayer version is expanded in a delightful way, the grass is 'tender' and the streams 'gently passe'.

The third verse in Herbert's version very much reflects his own experience. He had known what it was to 'stray', and he had known what it was to turn again, to 'convert', from the Latin *convertere*, to turn about. Particularly revealing is the phrase 'and bring my mind in frame'. We know Herbert liked everything neat and in order. We can imagine his mind and emotions at one stage all over the place and then becoming calm as he resettled himself in God, his mind once more in frame, its framework strong and, as we might say, 'in a good frame of mind'. Then there is the great Reformation emphasis, which he passionately believed, that this was only the result of grace, not anything he deserved as a result of his efforts.

In the fourth verse, Herbert changes 'the valley of the shadow of death' to the slightly less forbidding 'death's shady black abode' and gives a bolder nudge to the walker through it: 'Well may I walk, not fear'. This poem was not in *W* so was probably written in the later part of Herbert's life when as a result of severe illness he was conscious of death. So it was a poem of reassurance for himself.

In the next verse, the meal is grander than in the Book of Common Prayer version. The poet is sitting at table and dining, and his glass is filled with wine. Herbert enjoyed many fine meals with his hospitable mother and stepfather, but what he primarily has in mind of course is the heavenly banquet, of which the Eucharist is a foretaste. All Christians have a place at this table already laid for them. Those who reject the invitation to dine can only look on with envy. Oil was used for anointing kings, as it was in the coronation of King Charles III, and also on other special occasions as a mark of particular favour. The container for the oil and the cup for the wine are not just filled to the brim; they are brimming over. The divine grace and favour are without limit.

The final verse begins with a lovely phrase, 'Surely thy sweet and wondrous love', followed by a very Herbertian image: 'Shall measure all my days'. Again, the idea of exactness, of order, but perhaps also with the poetic and musical meaning of 'measure' as defined by the Oxford English Dictionary: 'Rhythmical motion, especially as regulated by music'. So our daily rhythm when properly ordered is at one with the divine music. Herbert then changes the imagery of being in the Lord's house to something that again was so characteristic of him: a life of praise, which nothing will stop.

In this wonderful psalm we have all that is needed for a human existence. In the first two verses God is with us in all our good times.

In the third he is with us when we stray and in the fourth as we die, assuring us that God is there in these dark times as well. The fifth verse looks beyond this life and gives us a wonderful hope, and the final verse simply sings about this 'sweet and wondrous love'.

The version in the Book of Common Prayer, by Myles Coverdale reads:

1  THE LORD is my shepherd: therefore can I lack nothing.
2  He shall feed me in a green pasture: and lead me forth beside the waters of comfort.
3  He shall convert my soul: and bring me forth in the paths of righteousness, for his Name's sake.
4  Yea, though I walk through the valley of the shadow of death, I will fear no evil: for thou art with me; thy rod and thy staff comfort me.
5  Thou shalt prepare a table before me against them that trouble me: thou hast anointed my head with oil, and my cup shall be full.
6  But thy loving-kindness and mercy shall follow me all the days of my life: and I will dwell in the house of the LORD for ever.

# Friday
# The collar

I struck the board, and cried, 'No more;
    I will abroad!
What? shall I ever sigh and pine?
My lines and life are free, free as the road,
Loose as the wind, as large as store.
    Shall I be still in suit?
Have I no harvest but a thorn
To let me blood, and not restore
What I have lost with cordial fruit?
    Sure there was wine
    Before my sighs did dry it; there was corn
    Before my tears did drown it.
 Is the year only lost to me?
    Have I no bays to crown it,
No flowers, no garlands gay? All blasted?
    All wasted?
Not so, my heart; but there is fruit,
    And thou hast hands.
    Recover all thy sigh-blown age
On double pleasures: leave thy cold dispute
Of what is fit and not. Forsake thy cage,
    Thy rope of sands,
Which petty thoughts have made, and made to thee
    Good cable, to enforce and draw,
    And be thy law,
While thou didst wink and wouldst not see.
    Away! take heed;

I will abroad.
Call in thy death's-head there; tie up thy fears;
    He that forbears
    To suit and serve his need
    Deserves his load.'
But as I raved and grew more fierce and wild
    At every word,
Methought I heard one calling, *Child!*
    And I replied *My Lord.*

A collar is sometimes put round the neck of a dog or other animal to restrain it, as reflected in the saying 'To slip the collar', which means to become free of what is holding it. There may also be a pun on the word 'choler', meaning anger. Although Herbert came to be regarded as saintly, according to his brother he was not exempt from 'choler'. In this poem, that anger is given free rein as the poet raves against the thought of being a clergyman. The title could not, however, refer to a clerical collar, colloquially known as a 'dog collar', because these were not worn until 1894. The poem is not in the earlier collection *W*, but it was clearly written before he had found peace of heart through his ministry at Bemerton.

There used to be a phrase in the army which summed up a rebellious soldier: 'He threw down his rifle and said, "I'll soldier no more."' This is what Herbert is doing here in banging his fist on the table and shouting that he has had enough and will go abroad. He wants to get away from it all and start a new life in another country. The fourth line finds him almost imagining himself as a man of the road, just going out and wandering where he wants, thinking himself free to do just what he wants, when he wants.

This is a poem in which form and content are perfectly matched. The lines, matching the state of rebellion, do not conform to any regular pattern. At the same time, they vividly convey not just an idea but an emotion. Take the opening:

I struck the board, and cried, 'No more;
   I will abroad!
What? shall I ever sigh and pine?
My lines and life are free, free as the road,
Loose as the wind, as large as store.
   Shall I be still in suit?

We can almost hear the bang on the table as well as the cry and feel the anger in both: 'struck' and 'cried' are like the cracking of a whip, while 'board', 'more' and 'abroad' stretch forward as though already leaving. All combine internal rhyming and alliteration, as do 'sigh' and 'pine'. Then we are brought up short with, 'Shall I be still in suit?', which vividly expresses and evokes a sense of constraint.

Then in line 7 he focuses on one complaint in particular: his life is so unproductive, nothing is coming to fruition. It was a particular complaint of Gerard Manley Hopkins as well, when he was going through a bad patch. Here Herbert remembers a time when there was corn and wine, images in the psalms of flourishing. But now not only has the last year been wasted, but also there are no garlands of victory to reward his efforts at the end of it.

While these verses express anger and a desire to be free, at the same time there is a hidden message coming through in the *double entendres*. The board he bangs is not just the one in the dining room, but also the Communion table. The thorn brings to mind the crown of thorns, the blood that of Christ's sacrifice, the wine that of Holy Communion, which is our cordial fruit, and the corn that is made into the true bread, Christ himself. So the conclusion of the poem is, as it were, already present, hidden in the earlier lines.

Then from line 17 the poet plays devil's advocate and says he can make up for what he has lost with 'double pleasures', almost like an upright man having a male menopause and suddenly starting to live a life of dissipation. He can give up the whole idea of thinking some things right or fit and others not. He can burst out of his self-made cage. He can realise that the ropes that bind him are made of sand formed by his petty thoughts. So again he urges himself to go abroad. A death's-head was a picture or model of a skull used to frighten people. The poet is urged to call its bluff and tie up his fears. If he were to simply stay there, enduring his life as it was, he would deserve his load. He has the power to take his life in his own hands and do something different.

Then as his raving gets fiercer and wilder, he simply hears the word 'Child!', and he replies, 'My Lord.' When a child is sobbing with unhappiness, they are sometimes comforted by a parent just taking them into their arms and holding them close. Nothing needs to be said.

Perhaps Herbert as a child had experienced such gentle reassurance from his much-loved mother or one of her servants. Here he is not frightened of depicting himself as a child in relation to God, one in a state of total dependence and trust. Indeed, Jesus himself said that we must become like little children. As Herbert put it in his poem 'Holy baptism (2)', 'Childhood is health.'

As stated earlier, there are a number of poems expressing a sense of rebellion against God, of which this is the best. It is an experience that many Christians will have had at one time or another, in mild or strong form. Sometimes this comes about because of a too limited, and therefore distorted, view of God. God is the eternal, underlying ground of all that exists, the primary cause of all secondary causes. He is not one cause among many. He is not a thing in the world of things, an item in a list of items. Because he is God, in this sense, his reality is not a threat. In the case of finite things, it is often the case that the more there is of one, the less there is of others. This is not so with God: just the opposite. The more there is of God, the freer we are to be fully and truly ourselves. So one reason we might feel a sense of rebellion against God is because we have a wrong picture in our mind; we are thinking of a reality like other realities, which inhibits our freedom. A true picture of God does not block our freedom. Furthermore, if God is good, all good, our true and everlasting good, the more we are given over to God, the more we are on the way to realising our true good.

This having been said, there may be occasions when we are genuinely doing something we know to be wrong and the rebellion is indeed directed against the true God. Then again, there is the call of Christ to follow him, and that may indeed go against what we immediately want to do, so there is a genuine tussle. With Herbert there was indeed such a call, to be ordained, about which he had such mixed feelings and which indeed seemed to him to be a constraint on his life. Yet he came to discover, as so many have, that the service of God 'is perfect freedom', a phrase used in 'Morning Prayer' in the Book of Common Prayer.

We think of freedom as the choice to do one thing rather than another, and that is indeed an important understanding of choice. But the profounder sense emerges when we think of someone who is, say, a musician, when all their talents and energies are focused on what they most want to do. That is when they feel totally fulfilled, when they are doing what they believe they were made for. When serving their music and following their vocation, they experience real freedom. The freedom we find in God is not one thing among others, music rather than rugby, cooking rather than running. It embraces and includes all that we do, if we let it.

# Saturday
# The pearl

I know the ways of learning; both the head
And pipes that feed the press, and make it run;
What reason hath from nature borrowed,
Or of itself, like a good housewife, spun
In laws and policy; what the stars conspire,
What willing nature speaks, what forc'd by fire;
Both th'old discoveries and the new-found seas,
The stock and surplus, cause and history;
All these stand open, or I have the keys:
    Yet I love thee.

I know the ways of honour; what maintains
The quick returns of courtesy and wit;
In vies of favours whether party gains
When glory swells the heart and mouldeth it
To all expressions both of hand and eye,
Which on the world a true-love-knot may tie,
And bear the bundle wheresoe'er it goes;
How many drams of spirit there must be
To sell my life unto my friends or foes:
    Yet I love thee.

I know the ways of pleasure; the sweet strains
The lullings and the relishes of it;
The propositions of hot blood and brains;

What mirth and music mean; what love and wit
Have done these twenty hundred years and more;
I know the projects of unbridled store;
My stuff is flesh, not brass; my senses live,
And grumble oft that they have more in me
Than he that curbs them, being but one to five:
    Yet I love thee.

I know all these and have them in my hand;
Therefore not sealed but with open eyes
I fly to thee, and fully understand
Both the main sale and the commodities;
And at what rate and price I have thy love,
With all the circumstances that may move.
Yet through the labyrinths, not my grovelling wit,
But thy silk twist let down from heav'n to me
Did both conduct and teach me how by it
    To climb to thee.

As the title of the poem makes clear, it is based on Matthew 13:45, which, with the preceding verse making the same point, reads:

> The kingdom of heaven is like treasure hidden in a field, which someone found and hid; then in his joy he goes and sells all that he has and buys that field.
>     Again, the kingdom of heaven is like a merchant in search of fine pearls; on finding one pearl of great value, he went and sold all that he had and bought it.
> (Matthew 13:44–6)

These verses set out 'all that he had'. Mercantile imagery runs through the whole poem, but it is not money that the poet values but other riches in his life. In the first verse it is a life of scholarship, in the second verse it is life at court and in the third verse it is a life of sensuous pleasure.

The meaning of 'Pipes that feed the press, and make it run' is not immediately clear. It would be tempting to think of a printing press, which was still such an exciting development at the time, but type then was all set up by hand; there was no machinery involved. The suggestion of an olive or wine press does not really seem to fit. The most interesting idea is that it refers to the circulation of the blood, the pipes being the arteries and the press being the heart, which William Harvey had written about in 1628 in *On the Motion of the Heart and Blood.*

In the rest of the verse, he sets out how we learn some things from nature and others we devise by our own ingenuity. He mentions all the different kinds of study: law, political philosophy, astronomy, geography and history. It was a time of intellectual excitement as well as of discoveries: 'new-found seas'. As a clever academic, this whole world was his: 'All these stand open, or I have the keys.'

The second verse sets out the delights of life at the court, which had so much appealed to part of Herbert. The quick repartee, the gossip as to who was in or out of favour, the feeling of being important and part of an inner circle, the drinking and pledges of undying love. All this can lead to a bestowal of favour on someone, which is like a love-knot so enticing that they carry it with them wherever they go.

The third verse is particularly successful in celebrating the life of pleasure: 'the lullings and the relishes of it'. This includes his beloved music but also laughter and wit, the enthusiasms of youth and love, which he has known. In short, 'My stuff is flesh, not brass'. He is a man of the senses. He likes the feel of things, and to enjoy sounds and tastes, sights and smells. There are five senses; why should they be controlled by a solitary will?

At the end of each of these verses there is the simple statement, 'Yet I love thee.' And in the final verse this is unpacked. He knows the satisfaction of these three worlds; they are in his hand. So it is not with eyes closed, sealed as a hawk's eye would be in training, but with eyes fully open, knowing what he is doing, that he flies to God. He knows what he is getting and the price he is paying. But he also knows what the divine love has cost. Then, in a final twist, as though to eliminate any trace of self-satisfaction in his love of God, he affirms that it is only possible because God has let down a silken twist to enable him to climb up to heaven. It is only through grace that we can believe and love. It has been suggested that we have here a reference to the thread of Ariadne which enabled Perseus to find his way out of the Labyrinth, as well as to the story of Jacob's ladder, but while neither are necessary, the echoes of both enrich the feel and sense.

Commercial images run all the way through the poem, 'stock and surplus' line 8, 'quick returns' line 12, 'bear the bundle' line 17, 'propositions' line 23, 'projects' line 26, culminating in 'main sale', 'commodities' and 'rate and price' lines 34–5. All this spells out what is meant in the parable by 'all that he had'. But for Herbert, of course, it has nothing to do with money; it is the world of learning, life at court and sensual pleasures that he has before him in his hand, which, with eyes fully open, he puts aside in favour of the pearl of great price. The pearl is love; the love of God and the answering love in himself as he reaches up and holds that 'silk twist'.

In this poem, there is no criticism of the three worlds that are put aside. There is no self-blame, as in some other poems, that he has not fully put them aside but hankers after them. He simply recognises them for what they are, with all their attraction, but says in effect, 'Here is something even more worthwhile, supremely worthwhile, a pearl worth selling everything else to possess.' The response is the simple, unadorned, 'Yet I love thee.'

Week 3

# HELD BY CHRIST

# Monday
# The family

What doth this noise of thoughts within my heart,
    As if they had a part?
What do these loud complaints and puling fears,
    As if there were no rule or ears?

But, Lord, the house and family are thine,
    Though some of them repine.
Turn out these wranglers, which defile thy seat:
    For where thou dwellest all is neat.

First peace and silence all disputes control,
    Then order plays the soul;
And giving all things their set forms and hours,
    Makes of wild woods sweet walks and bowers.

Humble obedience near the door doth stand,
    Expecting a command;
Than whom in waiting nothing seems more slow,
    Nothing more quick when she doth go.

Joys oft are there, and griefs as oft as joys:
But griefs without a noise.
Yet speak they louder than distemper'd fears.
    What is so shrill as silent tears?

This is thy house, with these it doth abound:
    And where these are not found,

Perhapst thou com'st sometimes, and for a day;
   But not to make a constant stay.

The poem begins with a sense of indignation. The poet asks his thoughts what they think they are up to, making such a noise with their complaints and puling (whining), as though there were no rules in his household and no one to hear them.

Despite this, the second verse begins with a wonderful affirmation. This house and family, with all its varied voices wrangling and repining (discontented) is 'thine'. It belongs to God. But belonging to God it should be neat, and we know how Herbert loved to be clean, neat and tidy. The third verse continues the thought. As God's family first of all, there needs to be silence, and then a sense of order that 'plays the soul', rather like a musical instrument. At Bemerton, the 'set forms and hours' took shape in calling together the family and village twice a day for morning and evening prayer. Within the family itself, there was a regular ordered routine. As he put in in the *The Country Parson*, 'The parson is very strict in the governing of his house.'[1] It brings to the poet's mind the well-laid-out gardens of his stepfather and friends. Gardens in the Stuart period were designed to be symmetrical, with walks and rides and terraces expressing humanity's control over nature, as did the topiary. The wild wood of our inner turmoil similarly needs to be tamed to become 'sweet walks and bowers'.

The fourth verse draws on the picture of the great houses with which Herbert was familiar, where there would be porters standing around ready to open doors and do whatever was asked of them. The surprising element is the reference to this figure as 'she', but this is because the soul is usually depicted as feminine. In the psalms, the soul waits quietly on God, such as in Psalm 62. Nothing looks slower than this waiting on God, for there is no end of it. Nevertheless, if there is a clear lead, the soul follows with alacrity.

The next verse fully acknowledges the presence of both joy and grief in this lively household. But if it is truly ordered under God, the

88

griefs won't be making a great fuss. Others, however, will know that they are there, for 'What is so shrill as silent tears?' The early poetry of R. S. Thomas is about the hill farmers to whom he ministered in the early 1940s. He knows that they have hands that have bruised themselves on 'the locked doors of life', and that their hearts are full of 'gulped tears'.[2] The same deeply moving image is well caught in Studdert Kennedy's poem from the First World War, 'A soldier for his mate', about a soldier mourning his dead comrade:

There are many kinds of sorrow
In this world of Love and Hate,
But there is no sterner sorrow
Than a soldier's for his mate.[3]

The final verse of Herbert's poem returns to the point made earlier. For all its unruly emotions and conflicting thoughts, 'This is thy house'. It still belongs to God. And it may be that when the house is quieter and the soul is stilled, God does make his presence known. But perhaps it is just for a short stay.

There is a realism about this poem that is endearing. It clearly reflects Herbert's own early family with his strong, articulate mother and a lively relationship with his siblings, including his able elder brother. More than that, it reflects an honesty about his own conflicted self. It was not in *W* so was probably written in the later part of his life, perhaps in the unsettled period after he left Cambridge before going to Bemerton.

Some of us, like Herbert, love a regular rhythm and routine to our lives and are inclined to be put out if it gets disrupted too much. I am inclined to say, 'Find a good rut and get stuck in it.' But even if we feel our life is all over the place and our thoughts and feelings are running riot, we can, with Herbert, say, 'This is thy house.'

# Tuesday
# The flower

How fresh, oh Lord, how sweet and clean
Are thy returns! even as the flowers in spring;
    To which, besides their own demean,
The late-past frosts tributes of pleasure bring.
        Grief melts away
        Like snow in May,
    As if there were no such cold thing.


    Who would have thought my shrivel'd heart
Could have recovered greenness? It was gone
Quite underground; as flowers depart
To see their mother-root, when they have blown,
        Where they together
        All the hard weather,
    Dead to the world, keep house unknown.


    These are thy wonders, Lord of power,
Killing and quickening, bringing down to hell
    And up to heaven in an hour;
Making a chiming of a passing-bell.
        We say amiss
        This or that is:
    Thy word is all, if we could spell.


    Oh that I once past changing were,
Fast in thy Paradise, where no flower can wither!
    Many a spring I shoot up fair,

Offering at heaven, growing and groaning thither;
    Nor doth my flower
    Want a spring shower,
My sins and I joining together.

But while I grow in a straight line,
Still upwards bent, as if heaven were mine own,
    Thy anger comes, and I decline:
What frost to that? what pole is not the zone
    Where all things burn,
    When thou dost turn,
And the least frown of thine is shown?

And now in age I bud again,
After so many deaths I live and write;
    I once more smell the dew and rain,
And relish versing. Oh, my only light,
    It cannot be
    That I am he
On whom thy tempests fell all night.

These are thy wonders, Lord of love,
To make us see we are but flowers that glide;
    Which when we once can find and prove,
Thou hast a garden for us where to bide;
    Who would be more,
    Swelling through store,
Forfeit their Paradise by their pride.

The wonderful first verse of this poem immediately sets the tone of exaltation. The word 'fresh' still conjures up so much, and it is not surprising it is so often used in advertising today. Because Herbert likes clean, well-cut clothes, and because his senses are so sharp, the state of being 'sweet and clean' means much to him. The 'returns' are the times when God feels close, perhaps simply because they are periods when he feels good about life and himself. He compares the return of this feeling, after a period in the doldrums, to spring flowers, which are not only beautiful in themselves – their demean or demeanour – but their beauty seems enhanced by the earlier frost. This thought leaves him singing and almost dancing. It could be a song by Shakespeare:

> Grief melts away
> Like snow in May

In the second verse, he continues the analogy of his life with that of a flower, this time when his 'shrivel'd heart' seems like a bulb in winter, hidden in the earth. This is the flower's 'mother-root'. The feminine is significant, when we remember the deep love that Herbert has for his own remarkable mother.

The third verse bravely accepts that both these conditions, feeling on top of the world and feeling depressed, come from God. Furthermore, it is a cause for wonder that one state can pass to another so quickly. In those days the slow tolling of the church bell took place as a person was dying, not afterwards. Under God, this can quickly change to a joyous chiming. We make our human judgements about what is amiss, what we think is good for us and what isn't, but if we could rightly understand God's word, all would be well.

In the next two verses he longs for a time when he is past these fluctuating moods and growing in a garden that is always in bloom. He knows how easy it is to start off with good intentions. He also knows that when he goes astray, he is sorry about it, so that his tears of remorse are like a spring shower. But still things go wrong. God seems like the equator where all things burn up at his least frown.

Then we have what are perhaps my favourite lines in all Herbert:

> And now in age I bud again,
> After so many deaths I live and write;
> I once more smell the dew and rain,
> And relish versing.

Herbert feels old, even though he is only in his thirties when he writes these lines. But the point is that it once more feels good to be alive: 'I once more smell the dew and rain', the sensual and the spiritual coalescing in a way that C. S. Lewis later recommends in suggesting that we learn to read sensual pleasures as God's touch upon us.[1] But for Herbert, it is even more than this. Once more he is being creative, he relishes versing. The word 'relish' again has a strong sensual impact.

In the final verse he draws a lesson from this dying and budding again. It is to remind him of what the burial service says:

> Man that is born of a woman hath but a short time to live, and is full of misery. He cometh up, and is cut down, like a flower; he fleeth as it were a shadow, and never continueth in one stay.

We come into existence and then glide away. This is because we have an eternal home, a paradisiacal garden. To want immortality now, like Adam, would be to swell with pride and forfeit that end which God has prepared for us.[2]

Herbert has a strong sense of divine providence in every aspect of creation and in every detail of his own life. In relation to nature, he sets this out in his long poem, 'Providence', in which he shows how everything in the natural world serves a useful purpose. Everything is under the power and love of God, but he makes a crucial distinction when he writes:

> For either thy *command*, or thy *permission*
> Lay hands on all: they are thy *right* and *left*.

The first puts on with speed and expedition;
The other curbs sin's stealing pace and theft.

Nothing escapes them both; all must appear,
And be dispos'd, and dress'd, and tun'd by thee,
Who sweetly temper'st all. If we could hear
Thy skill and art, what music would it be!

Today, most of us would place more emphasis on God's permission than his command, because events have to be allowed to happen as part of the price for having a creation at all. Also, we would be much more reluctant to try to guess what the purpose of this might be for us personally. Herbert, however, in verse 5 of 'The flower', interprets the bad times as divine anger and God's 'frown'. We could still try to draw some lesson out of difficult times without at the same time thinking of them as signs of God's hostility. When we are going through a difficult period, this is not a sign of either God's anger or his displeasure. This is the way things are. But God's Spirit does work within us, seeing what good might come out of a particular experience and helping us to cooperate with the divine leading in responding to it. At the same time, it is important not to think that this difficult period has been specially designed by God to bring that good about. That bad period has come about for a number of reasons, and some of it may indeed be our fault, but it is not helpful to ask about God's purpose behind it. That is veiled in mystery. What we do know is that we can make acts of trust and hope and love now, and this is what God wants of us.

Through all the changes of circumstance and fluctuations of mood, Herbert reminds us in the last lines of 'The flower' that we are in the Garden of God's presence and providence. It is there we 'bide', or dwell.

# Wednesday
# The glance

When first thy sweet and gracious eye
Vouchsafed ev'n in the midst of youth and night
To look upon me, who before did lie
    Welt'ring in sin;
I felt a sug'red strange delight,
Passing all cordials made by any art,
Bedew, embalm, and overrun my heart,
    And take it in.

Since that time many a bitter storm
My soul hath felt, ev'n able to destroy,
Had the malicious and ill-meaning harm
    His swing and sway:
But still thy sweet original joy
Sprung from thine eye, did work within my soul,
And surging griefs, when they grew bold, control,
    And got the day.

If thy first glance so powerful be,
A mirth but opened and sealed up again;
What wonders shall we feel, when we shall see
    Thy full-eyed love!
When thou shalt look us out of pain,
And one aspect of thine spend in delight
More than a thousand suns disburse in light,
    In heav'n above.

We quite often glance at other people. Mostly this is out of curiosity to see who they are or what they are up to. Sometimes it is more than this. We glance at them because we are attracted to them and just want to look at them without it seeming too obvious. In this fine poem, which did not appear in *W* so was written somewhat later, Herbert contrasts God glancing at him during the time of his youthful Christian faith with the image of God looking at him with eyes wide open, with 'full-eyed love'. A fair number of Christians go through an early period of intense religious devotion, perhaps after an experience of conversion, or in a teenage religious phase, or at the time of a call to ordination or some other major Christian work. Herbert suggests that what God has in mind for us is something even more wonderful.

We know that even when he was young, Herbert was devout and very serious about his faith. This is clear, for example, from a letter to his mother when he was seventeen. At this time, he 'felt a sug'red strange delight'. Sugar in the early seventeenth century was much more of a luxury than it is now. Perhaps mixed with fruit it was superior to 'all cordials made by any art'. The root of the word 'cordial' is *cor*, the Latin word for 'heart'. And the point about cordials at the time was not just that they were a pleasant drink, but that they stimulated the heart and the whole system. At that time, Herbert gladly took it in. He rejoiced in that early devout phase.

It is also a familiar experience for most Christians, as it was for Herbert, that such periods of intense emotion do not last. He went through bad periods of inner storms and temptations, but the memory of his earlier experience kept him going. This enabled him to control his 'surging griefs'. As so often with Herbert, his poetic art, his stresses and rhymes, exactly convey the emotion he is expressing. In this second verse, for example, the 'swing and sway' of harm is vigorously countered with the rising up of 'sprung' and 'surging', followed by the definite 'control' and 'got the day'.

In the third verse he moves from the use of 'I' to 'we', from his personal experience to what all Christians can look forward to. His first glance is but a mirth. At the time, 'mirth' meant an entertainment or diversion – something short-lived. If this first glance brought such pleasure, what wonder there will be with 'thy full-eyed love'? A parent will look with adoring face at their newborn child; it will glow with love. So also lovers look into one another's eyes.

With this full-eyed love, 'thou shalt look us out of pain'. Again we think of a child who has hurt themselves being comforted by the parent who is holding and looking at them. The pain may still be there, but it is forgotten as they are taken into love. Perhaps here we see a clue to the ultimate mystery of how all the terrible suffering in human life could ever be justified. At the end there will be no more crying because all is caught up in a full-eyed love of such intensity that all else drops away.

Austin Farrer in a fine sermon took this image even further. However often I may turn my back on God, he forgives me, for:

> he takes my head between his hands and turns my face to his to make me smile at him. And though I struggle and hurt those hands – for they are human, though divine, human and scarred with nails – though I hurt them, they do not let me go until he has smiled me into smiling: and that is the forgiveness of God.[1]

In the Bible, the face of God is first of all something mortals cannot look on, indicating the utter otherness and unknownness of God in himself. But at the same time the believer prays that God will look on us and will not turn his face from us; these are familiar cries in the Psalms. Perhaps most helpful of all is the refrain from Psalm 80, which in the Common Worship version, reads:

> Turn us again, O God of hosts;
> Show the light of your countenance, and we shall be saved.

# Thursday
# A dialogue

SWEETEST Saviour, if my soul
   Were but worth the having,
Quickly should I then control
   Any thought of waving.
But when all my care and pains
Cannot give the name of gains
To Thy wretch so full of stains,
What delight or hope remains?

*What, child, is the balance thine,*
   *Thine the poise and measure?*
*If I say, 'Thou shalt be mine,'*
   *Finger not my treasure.*
*What the gains in having thee*
*Do amount to, only He*
*Who for man was sold can see;*
*That transferr'd th' accounts to me.*

But as I can see no merit
   Leading to this favour,
So the way to fit me for it
   Is beyond my savour.
As the reason, then, is Thine,
So the way is none of mine;
I disclaim the whole design;
Sin disclaims and I resign.

*That is all: if that I could*
  *Get without repining;*
*And My clay, My creature, would*
  *Follow My resigning;*
*That as I did freely part*
*With My glory and desert,*
*Left all joys to feel all smart –*


Ah! no more: thou break'st my heart.


Many poets have included dialogue in their poetry, but on the whole it is the give and take of conversation, as in Robert Browning's long poems in the nineteenth century and those of Edward Thomas in the twentieth. But in this poem of Herbert's, the dialogue has much more the nature of a dispute, and it has something of the form of a formal disputation that was such a feature of university life in Cambridge at the time. Undergraduates were examined not by exam but by how well they did in a disputation, in Latin, on a set subject that they were given, to argue for or against it, whatever their own views might be. They had to do two of these in their own college and two before the University. In addition, these disputations were regarded as a form of entertainment, so there would be extra ones for visiting royalty, for example. In this poem, the poet and Christ dispute with one another about the value of the poet himself, George Herbert. It follows the same pattern as 'Love (3)', in which Herbert's protests about his own unworthiness are eventually broken down by continued affirmations of divine love.

In the first verse, the poet says that if he were of any value he would not have any thoughts of waiving the possibility of heaven, but he knows that however hard he tries, he remains 'full of stains', so he has no hope. This is countered by Christ, in verse 2, saying that the poet is acting like a shopkeeper totting up his balance sheet. He should remember he belongs to God, and he should not finger God's money. The value of that can only be known by the man who was sold – by Judas for thirty pieces of silver – and that value was transferred to the human account, including the poet.

But in verse 3, the poet persists that he can see nothing in himself that deserves this favour. So, as he can see nothing, he leaves it to God, and he will back out of the whole design. He disclaims the whole scheme, and this means that sin also gives up its claim, for there can then be no judgement of him.

In the final verse, Christ says that his resigning would be fine if it were the right kind of resigning, not the one that the poet proposes, which is full of repining, that is, discontent and dissatisfaction. If it were the right kind of resigning, then 'My clay, My creature' would follow the divine example. Here we see the stress on 'My'. The poet belongs to God. That example is seen in the way God emptied himself of divine glory to share the life of his mortal creatures, with all its pain and anguish, clearly a line based on the early hymn in Philippians 2:1–11. To this, the poet can only say, 'Ah! no more: thou break'st my heart.'

Down the centuries, the Christian Church has never had a definitive statement of how Christ's death brings about human salvation. Instead, there have been a number of theories of the atonement, as they have been called, in which a particular image or analogy has been unpacked to show how it has brought about the oneness, the at-one-ment, between God and humanity, all of which have limitations. But in this poem of Herbert we actually see and experience how that oneness comes about, by breaking the human heart. The extent of divine love for her creatures, as shown in the Incarnation and cross, breaks down all our barriers, not only of pride but also of self-accusation. Austin Farrer wrote that if we ask what then did God do for our salvation, the answer is:

> In the saving action of the incarnation God came all lengths to meet us, and dealt humanly with human creatures... He came

among them, bringing his kingdom, and he let events take their human course. He set the divine life in human neighbourhood. Men discovered it in struggling with it and were captured by it in crucifying it. What could be simpler? And what more divine?[1]

We see that process at work in the mind of Herbert as expressed in this poem.

For many people today, Herbert's tendency to blame himself, to harp on about his sin and unworthiness, is unreal and unhealthy. We are taught to believe in ourselves, to have a sense of self-worth. From a Christian point of view, we *are* of supreme worth. As Desmond Tutu used to like saying, 'God loves each one of us as though we were the only person in the world.'[2] God wants us enough to have created us, to have died for us and to have us with him for eternity.

To be created is to have a life of one's own, and that includes a drive to live and thrive. This is essential to survival. If a baby does not reach out for its mother's milk, and later for food, it will die. If it does not learn to protect itself, it will not survive. Self-interest is a fundamental part of us and of all creation and therefore cannot be wrong in itself. But as human beings we are called to grow beyond this into a concern for others and a love of God. Made in the image of God, we are called to grow into his likeness. This is a painful process, and when it happens there is a kind of miracle. Anyone who is aware of this vocation and has accepted Christ's invitation to follow him will also be conscious of where we are on the path, how much more we need to do in yielding to his loving call. This is not meant to lead to a lot of beating of the chest or laments of unworthiness, but to simple self-awareness and desire for grace. The overriding reality, the supreme truth, is the divine love by which and in which we are held.

# Friday
# The hold-fast

I threaten'd to observe the strict decree
　　Of my dear God with all my power and might;
　　But I was told by one it could not be;
Yet I might trust in God to be my light.
'Then will I trust,' said I, 'in Him alone.'
　　'Nay, e'en to trust in Him was also His:
　　We must confess that nothing is our own.'
'Then I confess that He my succour is.'
'But to have nought is ours, not to confess
　　That we have nought.' I stood amaz'd at this,
　　Much troubled, till I heard a friend express
That all things were more ours by being His;
　　What Adam had, and forfeited for all,
　　Christ keepeth now, who cannot fail or fall.

This is one of Herbert's poems in which the title has no direct connection to the poem itself or reference to it, but whose import becomes clear at the end.

The word 'threaten'd' in the first line is puzzling. Why should anyone want to threaten God by trying to obey him wholeheartedly? The word 'threaten' at the time had the same connotations as it does now, implying some intimidation by force or pressure. So the word must be being used paradoxically or ironically, almost playfully, as someone might say to us, 'You are being so nice I might even invite you to stay for a year,' and we reply, 'You are being so sweet I might even accept.' In each case there is humour, a humour only made possible because of the genuine affection of the couple.

This sets the tone of the poem. Some have seen the voice of the interlocutor in lines 3, 4, 6, 7, 9 and 10 as a dour Calvinist trying to squash any claim to human righteousness. But this is not necessarily the case. For at the heart of all Christian experience is the knowledge that we are radically dependent on God for all things. Moment by moment, our very existence comes from him, the ground of all being. So also any Christian attitudes or virtues we might exhibit come from him alone. God's grace is prevenient; it always goes before us and carries us along. It is a mistake to make this the basis of a rigid doctrine of predestination, as was done by Calvin, and indeed Augustine. But no Christian will deny the basic Christian experience that all is sheer grace. So each time in the poem when the poet says he will do something – first trust in God, then confess that nothing is our own – he is told he cannot even claim that to be his, not even the confession, for it is the having nothing, not the claim that we have nothing, that opens us fully to that grace.

The critical voice of the interlocutor can seem hard, but what it reveals is Herbert's acute self-awareness. He knows the vagaries of the human heart, how we never quite give up the attempt to justify ourselves. He knows that 'The heart is devious above all else' (Jeremiah 17:9). But in this poem that self-awareness does not go along with self-blame as it does in some other of his poems. It is a simple acknowledgement of reality: this is what all the children of Adam are like. As the penultimate line puts it, 'What Adam had, and forfeited for all'. Herbert is not concentrating on his own heart in isolation but on the condition of humanity, of which he is a part.

But then, in the final four lines, 'a friend' shares another paradox: 'That all things were more ours by being His'. How can things be all of Christ and at the same time all ours? That's just the way it is. The more it is of Christ the more it is ours. As the apostle Paul classically put it:

But by the grace of God I am what I am, and his grace towards me has not been in vain. On the contrary, I worked harder than

any of them – though it was not I, but the grace of God that is with me.
(1 Corinthians 15:10)

This means, as Paul also says, 'all things are yours' (1 Corinthians 3:21). This idea, that the whole world and everything in it belongs to us, was ecstatically expressed by another seventeenth-century poet, Thomas Traherne in his *Centuries of Meditations*.

So, in the final two lines, the poet is told that what Adam forfeited has been won back by Christ and is kept for the whole of humanity. We are now joined to and enclosed in his humanity, 'who cannot fail or fall'. A hold-fast is a clamp or bolt holding two parts of a structure together. What holds heaven and earth together, divine perfection and human frailty, is Christ. He is the clamp, the bolt, that holds fast through all earthquakes and floods and which cannot fail or fall. We seek to hold fast to this.

It is good for me to hold fast by God, to put my trust in the Lord God.
(Psalm 73:27, Book of Common Prayer)

# Saturday
# The pulley

When God at first made man,
Having a glass of blessings standing by,
Let us, said he, pour on him all we can.
Let the world's riches, which dispersèd lie,
    Contract into a span.

So strength first made a way;
Then beauty flowed, then wisdom, honour, pleasure.
When almost all was out, God made a stay,
Perceiving that, alone of all his treasure,
    Rest in the bottom lay.

For if I should, said he,
Bestow this jewel also on my creature,
He would adore my gifts instead of me,
And rest in Nature, not the God of Nature;
    So both should losers be.

Yet let him keep the rest,
But keep them with repining restlessness;
Let him be rich and weary, that at least,
If goodness lead him not, yet weariness
    May toss him to my breast.

Herbert could have used the account of creation in the Book of
Genesis. Instead, he draws his own picture of God with a great glass
of blessings which he wants to pour into humanity. I think of this not

as a drinking glass but as a great glass bowl full of fruit. From this glass flow all the goods we covet in life. Herbert is not a world-denier. He recognises that these are good things. Only one gift is withheld: peace of mind. This is because if human beings had all they wanted of material goods, it would be all too easy for them to rest content with these. So God lets humanity keep all the blessings of life, except one, so that if we do not turn to God out of gratitude we will at least turn to him in our discontent.

The word 'pulley' is not actually mentioned in the verse. The image called to mind is of a rope going round a pulley with a bucket at each end. A bucket of rubble goes down and the other bucket goes up. If the heavy weight is just allowed to drop, then the empty bucket on the other end of the rope will fly upwards. So the weight of human dissatisfaction with human pleasures taking us down will toss the bucket of our emptiness into God's breast.

There is a subtle play in the poem with the word 'rest'. In verse 2 it is rest in the sense of peace of heart and mind that is withheld from humanity. In verse 4, God allows humanity to keep the rest, that is the other blessings. But they keep them 'with repining restlessness'. Then, as in some other poems of Herbert, where the key word is hidden in the poem, the only place where true tranquillity can be found is in God's 'breast'.

The obvious background for the central theme of this poem was Augustine, in whose writings Herbert was well versed, and his famous prayer, 'You have made us for yourself, and our heart is restless until it rests in you.'[1] The Latin word is *quies*, quiet of mind. *Fecisti nos ad te et inquietum est cor nostrum, donec requiescat in te.* Our hearts are unquiet until they repose in God.

It has also been suggested that another possible reference is the myth of Pandora's box. In this story, Pandora, which means 'all gifts', was the first woman, sent by Zeus to punish Prometheus for creating and helping humanity. She had a storage jar or box in which all the evils of life were contained. This was inadvertently opened, and all the ills of life released except one: hope. In Herbert's version, of course, it is not the miseries of life that are in the storage jar, but its blessings, and what is withheld is not hope but rest.

'The religion of gratitude cannot mislead us,' wrote Wordsworth.[2] But the blessings of life do not always prompt a sense of thankfulness. Sometimes we take them for granted, even as a right. But we can also become satiated with them, sick and tired of them. Perhaps it is then that we discover there is something more to want.

The character of God in this picture is one of endearing humility. This is a God content to have humanity on any terms, even if it is only a weariness with the world's pleasures that tosses us to our true home. It is a picture not unlike that in Rose Macaulay's novel, *The Towers of Trebizond*, when the priest asks, 'How much longer are you going on like this, shutting the door against God?' The person addressed, who is caught up in a sinful relationship, is told:

> It will end: such things always end. What then? Shall you come back, when it is taken out of your hands and it will cost you nothing? When you will have nothing to offer God but a burnt out fire and a fag end. Oh, he'll take it, he'll take anything we offer. It is you who will be impoverished for ever by so poor a gift.[3]

Herbert himself was someone who had been given every possible gift: a loving home, intelligence, a good education, popularity, success, a creative wit. Worldly success had indeed been snatched away from him, but even before that, when he had it all, had he experienced that 'repining restlessness'? Is it true that if we have all we want of this world's goods – health, wealth, friends, fulfilment in work and love – then we would still find something missing? This is what C. S. Lewis found. He had a late marriage, and this convinced him that religion could not be manufactured out of our unconscious desire for sex. He and his wife had a fully satisfying sexual relationship.

Lewis said that, if God were a substitute for love, then his marriage would have resulted in losing all interest in him. But what both he and his wife discovered was that they wanted something in addition to each other. It was a different kind of want.[4]

The Christian conviction is that we find the meaning and purpose of our lives in and through our relationship with God. In him, the restlessness, agitation and dissatisfaction of life finds quiet of heart and lasting fulfilment.

Week 4

# ALL PRAISE

# Monday
## Love (1)

Immortal Love, author of this great frame,
    Sprung from that beauty which can never fade,
    How hath man parcel'd out Thy glorious name,
And thrown it on that dust which Thou hast made,
While mortal love doth all the title gain!
    Which siding with Invention, they together
    Bear all the sway, possessing heart and brain,
(Thy workmanship) and give Thee share in neither.
Wit fancies beauty, beauty raiseth wit;
    The world is theirs, they two play out the game,
    Thou standing by: and though Thy glorious name
Wrought our deliverance from th' infernal pit,
    Who sings Thy praise? Only a scarf or glove
    Doth warm our hands, and make them write of love.

## Love (2)

Immortal Heat, O let Thy greater flame
    Attract the lesser to it: let those fires,
    Which shall consume the world, first make it tame;
And kindle in our hearts such true desires,
As may consume our lusts, and make thee way.
    Then shall our hearts pant Thee, then shall our brain
    All her invention on Thine altar lay,
And there in hymns send back Thy fire again.

Our eyes shall see Thee, which before saw dust,
    Dust blown by wit, till that they both were blind:
    Thou shalt recover all Thy goods in kind,
Who wert disseized by usurping lust:
    All knees shall bow to Thee; all wits shall rise,
    And praise Him Who did make and mend our eyes.

These two poems really belong together, the first setting a challenge and the second answering it, so they will be considered in one reflection.

The first five lines of 'Love (1)' lament the fact that the word 'love', which truly belongs to God, is used most frequently of human love. And the early seventeenth century was very much a time for love poetry, especially that of Herbert's older friend John Donne in the early part of his life. But divine love is immortal, the creator of this great universe, 'This goodly frame, the earth'[1] and of unfading beauty. Herbert read and loved Augustine, who addressed God as 'beauty so old and so new'.[2] Instead of this being acknowledged, love was 'parcel'd out' and thrown on the dust which is humanity.

The next seven lines rub in the outrage. This human love engages our best efforts of heart and mind in clever repartee. 'Wit fancies beauty, beauty raiseth wit'. All the while this game is being played out before an admiring public, Divine Love, who rescued us from eternal fire, stands by, watching.

The poem ends on a challenge and lament:

Who sings thy praise? Only a scarf or glove
Doth warm our hands and make them write of love.

In 'Love (2)' this love is 'Immortal heat'. Dante, before Herbert, and T. S. Eliot after him, uses flame as a central image, a flame which is at once the burning pain of self-knowledge and the flame of divine love. This is the flaming light in which we both know ourselves and are rescued from ourselves. So the flame in the first five lines of Herbert's poem burns up our lusts, tames our hearts and kindles an answering flame of love in us which is drawn to the divine flame.

Line 6 echoes Psalm 42:1: 'As the hart panteth after the water brooks, so panteth my soul after thee, O God' (KJV), and then, with the way cleared to God, we can offer his gifts back to him again.

There is another expression of this thought in Charles Wesley's fine hymn:

> O thou who camest from above,
> The pure celestial fire to impart,
> Kindle a flame of sacred love
> On the mean altar of my heart.[3]

At this point our eyes are opened. The dust caused by the excitement of being witty and popular, which blinded them, is blown away. Then the goods of brain and invention which had been seized were recovered and were paid back 'in kind', as a neighbour might borrow some sugar and pay it back with sugar of a similar type. It continues:

> All knees shall bow to Thee; all wits shall rise,
> And praise Him Who did make and mend our eyes.

So Herbert ends with all our highest faculties utilised in his great theme of praise.

# Tuesday
# Jordan (I)

Who says that fictions only and false hair
Become a verse? Is there in truth no beauty?
Is all good structure in a winding stair?
May no lines pass, except they do their duty
    Not to a true, but painted chair?

Is it no verse, except enchanted groves
And sudden arbours shadow coarse-spun lines?
Must purling streams refresh a lover's loves?
Must all be veil'd, while he that reads, divines,
    Catching the sense at two removes?

Shepherds are honest people; let them sing;
Riddle who list, for me, and pull for prime;
I envy no man's nightingale or spring;
Nor let them punish me with loss of rhyme,
    Who plainly say, *My God, My King.*

There are two poems with the title 'Jordan'. Jordan was, of course, the name of the main river running through the Holy Land, which was full of associations in both the Old and the New Testaments. More will be said at the end about its meaning in relation to the poem.

The word 'fiction' at the time meant not a novel but something made up, a fantasy, applied here to elaborate language about a loved one. Spiral staircases go back three thousand years and have a practical purpose, saving floor space. But they can also be very attractive and are perhaps put in sometimes simply for that reason. The lines suggest that a straightforward up and down set of stairs can be both practical and beautiful. The painted chair here is a throne, and refers to one depicted in a painting or on a mural.

The first verse draws on the imagery of a house and its furniture. The second on the imagery of a landscaped garden with its carefully cultivated woods, shelters and streams. In such landscapes there can be shady places that give way to lovely views, like much poetry where the meaning is at first hidden. The poet asks if this must always be so. Can't poetry be much more straightforward, saying what it means clearly?

The last verse begins by invoking the shepherds in the nativity scene who not only heard the angels sing but also 'returned, glorifying and praising God for all they had heard and seen, as it had been told them' (Luke 2:20). The poem continues by saying that other people can do what they want (list), make riddles or draw for a winning hand in the game of primero. As 'for me' there is no envy:

> Nor let them punish me with loss of rhyme,
> Who plainly say, *My God, My King.*

As in some other poems, the ending nicely turns the table on what has gone before. For here we have a nice rhyme combined with stark clarity and simplicity. Many readers will be reminded of a poem of Herbert's which is a famous hymn:

> Let all the world in every corner sing,
> *My God and King.*

Herbert was not alone in his quest for clarity and simplicity. Philip Sidney had published his popular *Astrophil and Stella* in 1591 and again in 1598, which depicts the poet suffering from writer's block and desperately searching for exotic and elaborate images. In response he is told:

Bring my truant pen, berating myself for spite,
'Fool', said my muse to me; look in thy heart and write.

'Jordan (2)' by Herbert also depicts a poet, this time not suffering from writer's block but 'thousands of motions in my brain did run' as he sought out 'quaint words and trim invention':

But while I bustled, I might hear a friend
Whisper, *How wide is this long pretence!*
*There is in love a sweetness ready penn'd:*
*Copy out only that, and save expense.*

Herbert, like Sidney, looked in his heart, and there he found the desire to praise divine rather than human love.

In a poem to be discussed later, 'A wreathe', the poet writes, 'Give me simplicity, that I may live'. Simplicity is not stupidity or naivety. Nor for many does it come easily. For some blessed few it comes naturally to their honest heart. For others it is the result of a lifetime's thinking, praying and striving. At the end of such a life a person might have achieved true simplicity. Herbert is a bit of a paradox, for while at Bemerton he did seem to achieve true simplicity of heart and life, he was still willing to use all his poetic gifts and arts to convey this in his verse, as for example we have seen with the ending of 'Jordan (1)'.

At the end of 'Little Gidding' T. S. Eliot suggests that, in every moment, there is the possibility of the Divine but, for this to be realised, a condition of 'complete simplicity' is necessary, and this costs 'not less than everything'. Behind these lines there is the teaching of Jean Pierre de Caussade, especially his theme of 'The Sacrament of the present moment'. We are to accept every moment as one in which God is present and abandon ourselves to his will in it. That is the simplicity that costs not less than everything.

# Wednesday
## A wreathe

A wreathed garland of deserved praise,
Of praise deserved, unto thee I give,
I give to thee, who knowest all my ways,
My crooked winding ways, wherein I live,
Wherein I die, not live: for life is straight,
Straight as a line, and ever tends to thee,
To thee, who art more far above deceit,
Then deceit seems above simplicity.
Give me simplicity, that I may live,
So live and like, that I may know thy ways,
Know them and practise them: then shall I give
For this poor wreath, give thee a crown of praise.

Wreaths have been made in Europe since the time of the Etruscans. In our own time, people often associate them with death, but their main significance in the past was as a sign of victory, as in ancient Greece where, made of olive leaves, a wreath would be put on the head of the victor in the Olympic Games. Sometimes the association with death and the sign of victory are combined, both in the ancient world and now, as in the Remembrance Sunday ceremony. This beautiful and highly crafted poem itself takes the form of a wreath, as will be explored later.

The poem is about praise, deserved praise, made even by someone whose ways are 'crooked' and 'winding'. A crooked and winding life is one that leads to death. Here, death means not just physical death, but death in the sense of being cut off from God. In the Hebrew Scriptures, the people are given the choice of life or death, true life, that is life in union with God. So in this poem in line 6 we have the alternative to death, which is a life that is 'Straight as a line, and ever tends to thee'.

The winding life is characterised by deceit and self-deception, for we are reluctant to properly know ourselves. This is in sharp contrast to the honest self-knowledge and simplicity of the truly good life. Here we have the line, 'Give me simplicity, that I may live', discussed in relation to an earlier poem. So the poet ends by asking that he might live like that, both knowing and practising the way of God. If that happens then he will 'For this poor wreath, give thee a crown of praise'. The point here is that the wreath is made by threading a branch in and out, which is the best we can do. But if we live it as true as we can it will be not just a garland to hang round the neck, which is such a frequent and lovely custom in India when someone is welcomed, but a chaplet that goes on the head, like the crown of thorns, but in this case 'a crown of praise'.

If we look back at the poem, we see it takes the form of a winding wreath, the last word of each line being repeated near the beginning of the next. Then, again the last word of each of the first four lines is repeated in the last four lines of the poem but in reverse order so that the 'deserved praise' of the first line comes to a climax in 'a crown of praise' in the last line. The whole poem, like our lives, is an interlacing but with the possibility of making a crown at the end. It is Herbert's poetic mastery at its highest, without losing the essential simplicity of his theme, which is praise. An extra musicality is given to the poem by the repeated use of the words give and live.

Herbert is above all a poet of praise. In a cynical age, praise does not come easily. There is, as W. B. Yeats put it in 'The seven sages':

A levelling, rancorous, levelling sort of mind
That never looked out of the eye of a saint
Or a drunkard's eye.

Praise begins in recognising something good, then appreciating and admiring it. It takes us out of ourselves as we focus on what is worthwhile in itself. Sometimes the good is so good we are astonished and lost for words. For those keen on tennis, it happened when Roger Federer was at his peak. It felt a privilege to have lived at a time when he played. Other people will be able to draw examples from elsewhere: perhaps ballet or football, music or gymnastics.

The main purpose of having minds like ours is to discover the things that are of real value, setting aside all shams, shows and stunts to know what will last. The kind of qualities we saw in the late Queen Elizabeth II, for example, which the country as a whole, even republicans, were able to recognise and praise.

Suppose we come to recognise that there is a reality that is good, all good, supreme good, our true and everlasting good. Then there would be praise indeed. Herbert recognised this reality, which is why he was a poet of praise who wanted to sing 'My God and King' all his days. Christopher Smart, who wrote a famous poem about his cat praising God, also wrote, in 1776, in his long praise poem 'A song to David':

Praise above all – for praise prevails;
Heap up the measure, load the scales,
    And good to goodness add:
The gen'rous soul her saviour aids,
But peevish obloquy degrades;
    The Lord is great and glad.

# Thursday
# Dullness

Why do I languish thus, drooping and dull,
    As if I were all earth?
O give me quickness, that I may with mirth
      Praise thee brim-full!

The wanton lover in a curious strain
    Can praise his fairest fair;
And with quaint metaphors her curled hair
      Curl o're again.

Thou art my loveliness, my life, my light,
    Beauty alone to me:
Thy bloody death and undeserv'd, makes thee
      Pure red and white.

When all perfections as but one appear,
    That those thy form doth show;
The very dust, where thou dost tread and go,
      Makes beauties here;

Where are my lines then? my approaches? views?
    Where are my window-songs?
Lovers are still pretending, & ev'n wrongs
      Sharpen their Muse:

But I am lost in flesh, whose sugared lies
    Still mock me, and grow bold:

Sure thou didst put a mind there, if I could
    Find where it lies.

Lord, clear thy gift, that with a constant wit
    I may but look towards thee:
*Look* only; for to *love* thee, who can be,
    What angel fit?

The broken rhythm of the first line well conveys the mood of its meaning. It brings to mind a flower hanging down for lack of water. 'Quicken' is a vivid word that appears often in the Psalms, especially in the phrase 'Quicken thou me according to thy word' (Psalm 119:25 KJV). We ask not just to be brought to life, or made lively, but to be made alive in relation to God and his purpose for us. If this were to happen, the poet would indeed be able to offer a praise brimming over with love and laughter.

The poem then goes on to ask in pained tones why it is that lovers use all their art to praise their beloved but so few poems are written in praise of God, a point first made in 'Love (1)'. In the earliest poem of Herbert to survive, preserved in Isaak Walton's *Lives*, he resolved to be someone who did do just that: 'my poor abilities in poetry shall be all and ever consecrated to God's glory':

Doth poetry
    Wear Venus' livery only? Only serve her turn?
    Why are not sonnets made for thee, and lays
Upon thine altar burnt? Cannot thy love
Heighten a spirit to sound out thy praise
    As well as any she?[1]

In 'Dullness', the focus is on curled hair. But for the poet, God is the object of devotion. 'Thou art my loveliness... beauty alone to me.' Until the Reformation, it was taken for granted that God was not only goodness and truth but also beauty. Herbert continues that tradition. This is, of course, a moral and spiritual beauty, but this is not unrelated to physical beauty because he is the source and standard of all earthly delights, whether of eye or ear. It is this beauty that draws us to God, a beauty shown above all in Christ's willingness to die for us, clearing all obstacles that block our relationship with God. Red and white are the lover's colours, as is mentioned for example in two places in Shakespeare,[2] but they are not so beautiful as the red and white of Christ's flesh and blood. In him are all perfections, and that is shown here on earth in the footsteps of his Incarnation.

Lovers sing their 'window-songs', the aubades that woke the beloved at dawn, with all their exaggeration of human beauty. Where are the window-songs for God? He might perhaps have looked to the psalms for help:

My heart is ready, O God, my heart is ready;
I will sing and give you praise.
Awake, my soul; awake, harp and lyre,
That I may awaken the dawn.
(Psalm 57:8–9, *Common Worship*)

In any case, 'the sugared lies' prompt him to do something. In the final, subtle lines he trusts that God has put a mind in him which will offer praise, but he cannot find it. What he can do, however, is look. For who can truly love God? He can't, but he can look. And that is in fact what the wisest of spiritual guides tell us. Whether we are exulting or drooping, it may be that what is required of us is simply to look to God and wait on him. 'On you alone, O Christ, my soul in stillness waits'.[3]

# Friday

# Joseph's coat

Wounded I sing, tormented I indite,
    Thrown down I fall into a bed, and rest:
Sorrow hath chang'd its note: such is his will,
Who changeth all things, as him pleaseth best.
    For well he knows, if but one grief and smart
Among my many had his full career,
Sure it would carry with it ev'n my heart,
    And both would run until they found a bier
    To fetch the body; both being due to grief.
But he hath spoil'd the race; and giv'n to anguish
One of Joys coats, 'ticing it with relief
To linger in me, and together languish.
    I live to shew his power, who once did bring
    My *joys* to *weep*, and now my *griefs* to *sing*.

'Wounded' and 'tormented' are very strong words. They indicate the intensity of the pain being experienced. Yet the poet proclaims that even when wounded he sings, even when tormented he indites. The word 'indite' has for us an accusatory tone, but in Herbert's time it meant to put into words, as we see in Milton and Psalm 45 in the Book of Common Prayer: 'My heart is inditing of a good matter.' This suffering is so debilitating that all he can do is fall back into his bed. But there, 'Sorrow hath chang'd its note'. Herbert was fascinated by the way music could bring about change, turn feelings into something else. Here, grief and hurt are given a new note. If left to themselves, they would have swept his heart along with them and then both heart and body would race to the grave. 'But he hath spoil'd the

123

race'. Anguish has been given a new clothing, Joseph's coat of many colours, one of them being joy. Joy entices grief to stay and linger rather than hurry to the grave. So it is that as happiness can quickly turn to weeping, so grief can begin to sing, for all is within the good care of divine power and wisdom.

Everyone's life is a mixture of good fortune and bad, happiness and sadness, pleasure and pain. As William Blake put it in 'Auguries of innocence':

> Joy and woe are woven fine
> A clothing for the soul divine
> Under every grief and pine
> Runs a joy with silken twine

Herbert calls this clothing 'Joseph's coat', the point being that Joseph was the beloved son:

> Now Israel loved Joseph more than all his children, because he was the son of his old age: and he made him a coat of many colours.
> (Genesis 37:3 KJV)

Although this mixture of joy and woe often does not feel like the product of a wise and loving power, it is in fact the clothing of one who is deeply loved.

For the most part we associate song with happiness. We sing when we are cheerful. How can we sing when we are down in the dumps? Clearly it has to be a different kind of song, and there is of course much music that expresses sadness. It is not helpful to try to force oneself, let alone others, to be cheerful when they are feeling just the opposite. That's why platitudes about clouds with a silver lining, calls to 'cheer up' and a set rictus smile grate. During the exile in Babylon in the sixth century BCE, the psalmist asks, 'How could we sing the

LORD's song in a foreign land?' (Psalm 137:4). He knew he could not sing songs of jubilation, but the psalm itself is a song to the Lord, albeit in a sad key.

Irrespective of one's own personal mood at any particular time, anyone who is sensitive will have a sense of sadness, anger and sometimes despair about the state of the world with all its tragedy, suffering, cruelty and injustice. Believers may well say, 'How could we sing the Lord's song in a foreign land?' For some, the only answer lies in the Jesus Prayer or a variation of it: 'Lord Jesus Christ, Son of God, have pity on your world.' In the Eucharist, the same sentiment is expressed when we sing or say the Agnus Dei, when we bring the pity of the suffering Lamb of God to bear upon our broken world.

The central character in Stephen Beresford's play *The Southbury Child* is a vicar who is something of a failure. He drinks, he has not been faithful, and the parish is united against him because, for once making a stand on principle, he won't give a bereaved mother the balloons she wants at her child's funeral. But at least he knows he is a failure. A particularly moving moment occurs near the end when he simply stands with a sense of helplessness and prays the Jesus Prayer.

The prayer of the Church is prayer for a failed world. But this prayer can be a kind of music: sad, haunting but lifting grief into a new plane.

In his poem 'East Coker', T. S. Eliot writes of 'the wounded surgeon', and in recent years the phrase 'the wounded healer', which originated with Carl Jung, has become more widely known as the title of a book by Henri Nouwen. It is often those who are wounded who are best able to come close to the wounds of others. 'Wounded I sing,' Herbert begins, and ends, 'And now my *griefs* to *sing*'.

# Saturday

# Christmas

After all pleasures as I rid one day,
    My horse and I, both tired, body and mind,
    With full cry of affections, quite astray;
I took up the next inn I could find.
There when I came, whom found I but my dear,
    My dearest Lord, expecting till the grief
    Of pleasures brought me to Him, ready there
To be all passengers' most sweet relief?
Oh Thou, whose glorious, yet contracted light,
    Wrapt in night's mantle, stole into a manger;
    Since my dark soul and brutish is Thy right,
To man of all beasts be not Thou a stranger:
    Furnish and deck my soul, that Thou mayst have
    A better lodging, than a rack, or grave.


The shepherds sing; and shall I silent be?
    My God, no hymn for Thee?
My soul's a shepherd too; a flock it feeds
    Of thoughts, and words, and deeds.
The pasture is Thy word: the streams, Thy grace
    Enriching all the place.
Shepherd and flock shall sing, and all my powers
    Out-sing the daylight hours.
Then will we chide the sun for letting night
    Take up his place and right:
We sing one common Lord; wherefore he should
    Himself the candle hold.

I will go searching, till I find a sun
    Shall stay, till we have done;
A willing shiner, that shall shine as gladly,
    As frost-nipped suns look sadly.
Then will we sing, and shine all our own day,
    And one another pay:
His beams shall cheer my breast, and both so twine,
Till ev'n His beams sing, and my music shine.

This consists of two sonnets. The first was included in *W*, the second was not and so was presumably written later.

Herbert, as an aristocrat, would have known all the pleasures of horse riding, and during the Christmas period the hunts would have been out in force. The poem imagines him out in such a hunt, but the dogs have gone off course and their baying has led horse and rider 'quite astray'. Indeed, so far from home are they that they put up at the nearest inn they can find. It is not just the horses that have gone astray, but also the rider pursuing 'all pleasures' who has followed his 'full cry of affections'.

In the inn he was amazed to find his dear Lord waiting patiently for him. Was he waiting for 'the grief of pleasures' to bring him there for 'sweet relief'? This might refer to being so satiated with pleasure that the person is sick and tired of it, or more specifically to finding some deeper restlessness that needs to be satisfied, as in 'The pulley'. Either way, it is a lovely picture of a God who does not force us but who waits patiently until we find our need of him.

In the stable of this inn, the glorious light behind the universe is contracted. Another seventeenth-century poet, Richard Crashaw, wrote of 'Eternity shut in a span',[1] and in the next century Charles Wesley wrote a hymn with the line, 'Our God contracted to a span'.[2] The glorious light used the darkness of night to steal unseen into a manger. In that stable are animals. But humanity, dark and brutish though it may be, also belongs to God by right, so the poet pleads with God not to be a stranger to him.

Then, in the final two lines of the first sonnet, the poet asks that his soul might be furnished and decked as much as houses are at this time of year as they are made ready for Christmas. He asks that this house might be a better place to dwell than either a torture rack (the cross) or a grave.

In these verses, the imagery of the Christmas lessons are very much to the fore. The great prologue to St John's Gospel, for example, in which are the words:

In him was life; and the life was the light of men.
And the light shineth in darkness; and the darkness comprehended it not...
That was the true Light, which lighteth every man that cometh into the world.
(John 1:4–5, 9 KJV)

This would have been responded to in the Nicene Creed, in which Christ is described as 'Light of light'. Then there is the reference to the beasts, the ox and donkey, which appear in early depictions of the scene. As it was a stable they would have been there anyway, but from the standpoint of the early Christians it was a reference to Isaiah 1:3 where they are mentioned.

The poem particularly brings to my mind the painting 'The nativity at night' by Geertgen tot Sint Jans in the National Gallery, in which the Christ child in the crib is so luminous he lights up not only the faces bending over, but also the angels in the sky, all against a pitch-black background.

The first part of the second sonnet takes up the imagery of Luke's account of the nativity in chapter 2 with its wonderful vision of the angels singing, 'Glory to God in the highest, and on earth peace, good will toward men', and the shepherds who returned after seeing the Christ child 'glorifying and praising God' (Luke 2:14, 20 KJV). This leads into the thought that Herbert himself is a shepherd with a responsibility for his flock of thoughts, words and deeds. Here the poem draws on the imagery of Psalm 23, with the pasture being the word of God in the Bible and streams the streams of divine grace. So both shepherd and his flock of thoughts, words and deeds will sing.

The imagery then returns to that of light, with the poet teasing the sun for allowing night to fall and urging that it should act as a candle lighting up the sky all the time. If the sun won't do this, he will look for 'a willing shiner' who would shine as gladly as the sun looks forlorn on a frosty winter day.

The final four lines bring together light and music in a wonderful reciprocity. The sunbeams will make him cheerful so that light and music will interthread in one twine, 'Till ev'n His beams sing, and my music shine'. It is a wonderful example of what Charles Williams called co-inherence, when we take on ourselves the qualities of others.

Once again, all leads up to Herbert's great message of unceasing praise, a particularly appropriate theme for Christmas.

# Notes

## Introduction

1 Adam Nicholson, *Power and Glory: Jacobean England and the making of the King James Bible* (London: Harper Perennial, 2004), p. 1.

2 Izaak Walton, *The Life of George Herbert*, in Ann Pasternak Slater (ed.), *George Herbert: The Complete English Works* (New York: Everyman's Library, 1995), pp. 345–6. Cited as *Life* in *Works*.

3 John Aubrey, *Brief Lives*, ed. by Richard Barber (London: The Folio Society, 1975), p. 144.

4 Walton, *Life* in *Works*, pp. 360–1.

5 The poem goes on in less flattering terms: 'But name not winter faces, whose skin's slack / Lank as an unthrift's purse, but a soul's sack'. For this reason, Katherine Rundell thinks that either he badly miscalculated what would please or it was not written for her. Katherine Rundell, *Super-Infinite: The transformations of John Donne* (London: Faber & Faber, 2022), p. 167. However, Magdalene and Donne could hardly have been such close spirits unless she shared something of his brutal realism about death, and the poem ends on a positive note: 'I shall ebb out with them, who home-ward go.'

6 Walton, *Life* in *Works*, p. 342.

7 Funeral Sermon on Magdalene Herbert, Lady Danvers, 1627, in John Hayward (ed.), *John Donne: Complete Poetry and Selected Prose* (The Nonesuch Library) (London, New York: The Bodley Head, 1962), p. 569.

8 Aubrey, *Brief Lives*, p. 96: 'His complexion so beautiful and fine… that people would come after him in the street to admire him.' He 'was wont in fair mornings in the summer to brush his beaver-hat on the hyssop and thyme, which did perfume it with a natural

spirit and would last a morning or longer'.

9 Funeral Sermon, pp. 570–1.

10 Frank Kermode (ed.), *T. S. Eliot: Selected Prose* (London: Faber & Faber), 1975, p. 184.

11 Andrewes will have used the Bishops' Bible, which provided the base text for the King James Bible, shortly to be authorised, but is slightly different.

12 Richard Harries, 'Lancelot Andrewes' Good Friday 1604 sermon', in Michael Hattaway (ed.), *A New Companion to English Literature and Culture*, vol. 1 (Sussex: Blackwell, 2010), pp. 430–7.

13 George Herbert, *The Country Parson*, in Ann Pasternak Slater (ed.), *George Herbert: The Complete English Works* (New York: Everyman's Library, 1995), p. 217. Cited as *Parson* in *Works*.

14 R. S. Thomas (ed.), *A Choice of George Herbert's Verse* (London: Faber & Faber, 1967), p. 16.

15 Walton, *Life* in *Works*, p. 352.

16 Herbert, *Parson* in *Works*, p. 236.

17 Herbert, *Parson* in *Works*, p. 246.

18 Walton, *Life* in *Works*, p. 352.

19 Herbert, *Parson* in *Works*. p. 209.

20 Samuel Taylor Coleridge, letter to Lady Beaumont, 18 March 1826.

21 John Drury, *Music at Midnight: The life and poetry of George Herbert* (London: Penguin, 2014), p. 339.

22 Christopher Smart (1722–71), 'Adoremus'.

## The affliction (I)

1 Gerald Manley Hopkins (1884–89), 'Thou art indeed just, Lord, if I contend'.

## The sinner

1 Valerie Eliot and John Haffenden (eds), *The Letters of T. S. Eliot, Vol 4: 1928–1929* (London: Faber & Faber, 2013), p. 572. See also p. 567.

## Prayer (I)

1 William Shakespeare, *The Tempest*, Act 2, Scene 2.

## Love (3)

1 Simone Weil, *Waiting on God* (Glasgow: Fontana, 1969), p. 35.

2 Weil, *Waiting on God*, pp. 35–6.

3 George Herbert, *The Country Parson*, in Ann Pasternak Slater (ed.), *George Herbert: The Complete English Works* (New York: Everyman's Library, 1995), p. 228. Cited as *Parson* in *Works*.

4 Herbert, *Parson* in *Works*, p. 251.

## Redemption

1 R. S. Thomas (ed.), *A Choice of George Herbert's Verse* (London: Faber & Faber, 1967).

## The call

1 'Burial of the Dead', Book of Common Prayer.

## The family

1 George Herbert, *The Country Parson*, in Ann Pasternak Slater (ed.), *George Herbert: The Complete English Works* (New York: Everyman's Library, 1995), p. 210.

2 R. S. Thomas, 'The dark well', *Collected Poems* 1945–90 (London: J. M. Dent, 1993), p. 96.

3 Studdert Kennedy (1883–1929), 'A soldier for his mate'.

## The flower

1 Lewis said that, if he could always be what he aimed at being, then even the most ordinary pleasures would be transformed, from the

first breath of fresh air in the morning to soft slippers at bedtime. C. S. Lewis, *Prayer: Letters to Malcolm* (London: Fount, 1977), p. 91. See also Richard Harries, *C. S. Lewis: The man and his God* (London: Fount, 1987), p. 66.

2 D. H. Lawrence also compares his life with a plant in his poem 'Shadows', discussed in Richard Harries, *Hearing God in Poetry: Fifty poems for Lent and Easter* (London: SPCK, 2021), pp. 168–70.

## The glance

1 Austin Farrer, 'All Souls' Examination', *Said or Sung* (London: Faith Press, 1964), p. 68.

## A dialogue

1 Austin Farrer, *Saving Belief: A discussion of essentials* (London: Hodder & Stoughton, 1967), p. 99.

2 Desmond Tutu, no known written source.

## The pulley

1 Augustine of Hippo, *Confessions*, I.i.1, trans. by Henry Chadwick (Oxford: Oxford University Press, 1992), p. 3.

2 William Wordsworth, letter to Sir George Beaumont, 28 May 1825.

3 Rose Macaulay, *The Towers of Trebizond* (London: Collins, 1956), pp. 71–2.

4 C. S. Lewis, *A Grief Observed* (London: Faber & Faber, 1966), p. 10.

## Love (1) and Love (2)

1 William Shakespeare, *Hamlet*, Act 2, Scene 2.

2 Augustine of Hippo, *Confessions*, X.xxvii.38, trans. by Henry Chadwick (Oxford: Oxford University Press, 1992), p. 201.

3 Charles Wesley (1707–88), 'O thou who camest from above'.

## Dullness

1 Izaak Walton, *The Life of George Herbert*, in Ann Pasternak Slater (ed.), *George Herbert: The Complete English Works* (New York: Everyman's Library, 1995), p. 344.
2 'Venus and Adonis', line 10; *Love's Labour's Lost*, Act 1, Scene 2, line 90.
3 Author's own words, based on Psalm 62.

## Christmas

1 Richard Crashaw (1612–49), 'In the holy nativity of our Lord'.
2 Charles Wesley (1707–88), 'They shall call his name Immanuel'.

# Copyright acknowledgements

# Read on for an extract from *Majesty*

## by Richard Harries

Reflections on the Life of Christ
with Queen Elizabeth II

# Majesty

FEATURING FIFTY BEST-LOVED PAINTINGS,
FROM THE NATIVITY TO THE RESURRECTION

## RICHARD HARRIES

# 1
# LIGHT OF THE WORLD

'St Paul spoke of the first Christmas as the kindness of God dawning upon the world. The world needs that kindness now more than ever.'

**The Queen's Christmas broadcast, 1997**

DETAIL FROM
**THE ADORATION OF
THE SHEPHERDS**
Jacopo Bassano (1510–92)
King's drawing room,
Kensington Palace

# The annunciation

In the sixth month, the angel Gabriel was sent by
God to a town in Galilee called Nazareth, to a
virgin engaged to a man whose name was Joseph,
of the house of David. The virgin's name was
Mary. And he came to her and said, 'Greetings,
favoured one! The Lord is with you.' But she was
much perplexed by his words and pondered what
sort of greeting this might be. The angel said to
her, 'Do not be afraid, Mary, for you have found
favour with God. And now, you will conceive in
your womb and bear a son, and you will name
him Jesus. He will be great, and will be called the
Son of the Most High, and the Lord God will
give to him the throne of his ancestor David. He
will reign over the house of Jacob for ever, and of
his kingdom there will be no end.' Mary said to
the angel, 'How can this be, since I am a virgin?'
The angel said to her, 'The Holy Spirit will come
upon you, and the power of the Most High will
overshadow you; therefore the child to be born
will be holy; he will be called Son of God. And
now, your relative Elizabeth in her old age has
also conceived a son; and this is the sixth month
for her who was said to be barren. For nothing
will be impossible with God.' Then Mary said,
'Here am I, the servant of the Lord; let it be
with me according to your word.' Then the angel
departed from her.

**From the Gospel of Luke, chapter 1**

**THE ANNUNCIATION**
Carlo Maratti (1625–1713)
Queen's private chapel,
Hampton Court Palace

The annunciation was depicted in the fifth century, in a mosaic, and may even have been painted earlier than this in the catacombs. By the time of Fra Angelico in the fifteenth century it was a familiar scene in art. Fra Angelico was a monk and his version exudes quiet prayerfulness.

The version here by Maratti could not be more different. It is dramatic, even theatrical. The angel Gabriel, a towering figure with right arm raised, appears overpowering. Angels and putti are all around but almost pushed aside. Mary to the left looks up at him with a sense of surprise and questioning. Gabriel carries a white lily, the traditional symbol of Mary, who wears blue, her traditional colour, and is shown reading a book. It is open at Isaiah 7.14–16 (AV): 'Therefore the Lord himself shall give you a sign; Behold, a virgin shall conceive, and bear a son, and shall call his name Immanuel.'

The Holy Spirit, symbolized as a dove, overshadows Mary. The face of God the Father in outline looms above – which is incorrect theologically. According to Christian theology, God in himself is totally unknown and incomprehensible so should not be depicted in art. But God has made himself known in a way that we humans can understand, in Jesus, the Word made flesh. It is his life that justifies Christian art.

Maratti's version reflects two main influences, one religious and the other artistic. In response to the Protestant Reformation, the Roman Catholic Church made strenuous attempts to reform its life, known as the Counter-Reformation.

Religious orders were founded and missionaries went all over the world, inspired with a new zeal. Their preaching was dramatic, and they used theatre to get their message across. Although Maratti stood in the Classical tradition of Raphael, he was influenced by the much more flamboyant Baroque art. It is an art designed to depict, and get the viewer to share, strong emotions. So one of its features is light and glory, very much to the fore here with light breaking through the clouds and lighting up the darkness below. And it is right for it to be dramatic, for what could be more astounding than the Eternal Word taking form as a human person? What more glorious than Eternal Love sharing human vulnerability?